GONE BEFORE US

A Series of Reflections on the Mystery of Death, Grief and Life After Death

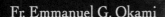

Fr. Emmanuel G. Okami

ISBN:
979-851-347-258-2

*****

EDITOR

Lisa Timms
Our Lady of Peace Parish, Burnham, UK.

*****

Printed by:
Floreat Systems
Catholic Archdiocese of Benin Printing Press
30, Airport Road,
Benin City, Edo State, Nigeria

I dedicate this book to
all those who have died
of COVID-19
and to all those who
are grieving.

* * * * *

FOREWORD

Death is an unpleasant subject. Unless someone is in the death business (i.e., mortuaries, cemeteries, tombstones, etc.), we usually don't like to talk about it—or even think about our own demise.

When the writer of Psalms exclaimed: "The terrors of death are fallen upon me. Fearfulness and trembling have come upon me and horror has overwhelmed me" (Psalm 55:4-5), he expressed the sentiments of vast multitudes who have faced the prospect of death.

Bildad, Job's friend, characterised death as the "king of terrors" (Job 18:14). And the writer of

Hebrews spoke of those "who through fear of death were all their lifetime subject to bondage" (Hebrews 2:15).

Death is a mystery and people tend to shy away from talking about it. However, it is a necessary debt to be paid. Anyone who is born is old enough to die.

In this book, *Gone Before Us,* Fr. Emmanuel Okami makes bold to reflect about death, grief and suffering. He helps the ready to understand the mystery of death and why death is inevitable. The reflections are concise, easy to read, rich in content and can be used for meditations. Each reflection ends with a prayer, making it a spiritual exercise as it gives the reader the ability to pray about death, suffering and grief.

Fr. Emmanuel has reflected on the importance of preparing for one's death as one would prepare for a celebration. Heaven is our home and adequate preparation should be made. This book helps us understand how we can best prepare for death, in a way that allows us to confront the reality without fear.

As you read through this book on death, I pray that the Holy Spirit will enlighten your mind and your heart to know the shortness of our lives, so that we may gain wisdom of heart (Psalm 90:12).

Rev. Sr. Okonta Evelyn Mario EHJ
Administrator of St. Martin De Pores Primary Health Care Centre,
Abwa Mbangen Gboko Diocese, Benue state, Nigeria.

AUTHOR'S NOTE

This period has been a very challenging one for most of us. The funerals I have had within the space of a year and a half are more than all the funerals I have celebrated in the almost ten years since I became a priest. So many people are dealing with the pains of grief. So many people are asking questions.

Some are being forced to reflect on the existence of God, the meaning and purpose of life, what happens after life and the eternal destiny of their souls. These are questions people hitherto would not bother about.

Many people are battling with their faith and some are having some deep-seated emotional crises following the demise of someone they never expected would be taken away from them. Many people have died without preparation or the opportunity to set their house and their lives in order.

Sadly, many people who died recently didn't really enjoy the comfort of having their family members around - thousands died in isolation. Many who mourn could not be supported as they needed because the world at large is in global grief.

This book, *Gone before us*, is born out of my own personal reflection on the subject of death and life after death. It is not essentially an intellectual write up or a doctrinal treatise; it is a collection of inspired meditations prompted by events around me but written with openness to the Holy Spirit, whose revelation and guidance make the difference in our interpretation of our experiences.

In this book, I try to explain the mystery of death from the Christian perspective, establishing the fact that it is not altogether a tragedy. I also focused on the theme of grief, how to grieve as Christians and how to support those who grieve. There is a discourse on how to move on and embrace life again when someone we love is taken from us. Many of the reflections focus on eternal life, the joy of heaven and how we can overcome the fear and horror of death by a joyful contemplation of eternal happiness with God and the Saints in heaven.

The purpose of this book is to help us confront our fears, to put our pains in perspective, to sanitise our thoughts on death. This book is not meant to scare, upset or distress us by making us think of a subject matter we would rather not think of, rather, it is meant to encourage all those who mourn and to teach us all to prepare for the inevitable.

I believe that those whose ministry involved supporting those who grieve will find this book very helpful, those battling with grief will find in it comfort and truth, those who are asking questions will find answers and those who are living will not be deluded about life but will prepare for the inevitable, so that when it comes it won't be a shock or a tragedy.

May the reading of this book bring the reader, knowledge, confidence, consolation, awareness, encouragement, hope, faith and great support, especially when they need to hear the words of comfort from God in a quiet morning, a damp afternoon, a sober evening or a dark night.

Yours in His vineyard,

Fr. Emmanuel Gukena Okami
Word of Life Ministry, Milton Keynes, UK,
A Priest of Ilorin Diocese, Nigeria,
On Mission in Northampton Diocese, UK.

★★★★★

Reviews

Thank you to the Holy Spirit for showering His grace on Fr. Emmanuel, enabling him to write this book, *Gone Before Us.* We are all aware that death awaits us one day but get completely paranoid about how we will face that day. Our everyday sufferings and our sinful ways only add to this fear. Reading this book helped me contemplate on areas of my life that need improving, in order to fulfil God's purpose for my life. The book allows us to confront our fear of death, then changes that fear into an understanding of the purpose of our lives and helps us prepare for our last moments in this world. Being reminded that we are dust and will return to dust gives us hope that we're all invited into God's presence for the everlasting life. Meditating on biblical evidence at the start of each chapter gives us a deeper understanding of our lives on this earth and after death.

Jaxo Natarajan
Parishioner of Our Lady of Peace Parish,
Burnham, UK.

★★★★★

L et us thank Fr. Emmanuel Okami for partnering with the Holy Spirit to produce such an important book for this COVID season, when we are shaken up and face the one reality of our lives that we cannot escape. With characteristic humility and love, Fr. Emmanuel gently but firmly leads us, through Scripture, prayer and meditation, to deal with the death of loved ones and strangers, releasing them to the Lord. He also prepares us for the encounter for all encounters with the Beloved. There is no fear or judgement here - only an urgency born of love and mercy. Be prepared, wake up and be ready to go through the door of darkness and death and into the life of Him Who is Light.

Pauline Gray
St. Barnabas Cluster, Milton Keynes, UK.

★★★★★

The Holy Spirit has inspired Fr. Emmanuel Okami to write this book of reflections titled *Gone Before Us,* on the mystery of death, grief and life after death. The reflections offer us an opportunity to start a fresh life, to live a good life, both leading to a happy and holy death. Fr. Emmanuel helps us to evaluate our lives, using quotations from the Bible and asking us questions, such as 'If you were called home, would you be ready to meet your Redeemer?' He encourages us to evaluate life from our present state, emphasising the importance of making amends with people and with God and leading a holy life before leaving this world. He explains how we can work for the kingdom and remain in God, ending with a prayer after each reflection.

This book offers the reader knowledge, better understanding and hope when faced with the loss of a loved one or their own mortality and gives us the promise and comfort of our Heavenly father.

Mrs Anne D'Mello
Parishioner of St. Thomas Aquinas and All Saints Parish, Bletchley, UK.

★★★★★

This book, *Gone Before Us,* is timely, written when the world is facing a pandemic, with many people losing their loved ones. It is not just a book of human knowledge or understanding but a divine revelation from heaven. I do not believe that it is by chance that you are reading this book. For some, reading these pages will answer questions that you have had but didn't know whom to ask. Others will be challenged to move closer to God and find His plan for their lives.

It is my prayer that this book will help many to get over the fear of dying, stir their faith and give them a desire to deepen their relationship with Jesus.

Jesus said that He was not leaving us as orphans, but that He would ask His Father to give us a Counsellor to be with us forever (John 14:16). He desires to walk with us, talk to us and give us directions whilst on this earth. May the Lord bless you as you read and step into this divine revelation shared by Fr. Emmanuel Gukena Okami.

Jesus is the only reason that I live. Glory be to His name.

Catherine Waweru
Parishioner of Holy Redeemer Catholic Church,
Wexham, UK.

★★★★★

This book, *Gone Before Us*, by Fr. Emmanuel Okami, answers our major questions about death. The contents calm our fears and restore us to authentic love of God. This book moves from our temporality on earth to our finality in heaven, for those who authentically prepare for it. And now, with gratitude to the Holy Spirit who leads us to the complete truth of our existence, I recommend this book for our spiritual growth in watching and waiting for the time that is known to God alone, the hour of our death. Please read, practice and tell others.

Fr. Peter A. Wojuaye (Deogratias5)
Formator, Seminary of All Saints, Uhiele-Ekpoma, Edo State, Nigeria.

★★★★★

I enjoyed reading this book, *Gone Before Us*, by Fr. Emmanuel Okami and found it quite touching but pure truth. For anyone who is bereaved, this book is simply a must have! It answers most of the troubling questions that arise at such moments of grief.

Fr. Evaristus Abu
St. Agatha Catholic Church, Benin City, Edo State

★★★★★

GONE BEFORE US

A Series of Reflections on the Mystery of Death,
Grief and Life After Death

Fr. Emmanuel G. Okami

TABLE OF CONTENTS

- Life is a gift 1
- Living in the now 4
- Lessons from the grave 8
- The value of time 12
- Remember you are dust 16
- The fear of death 21
- Categories of death 23
- God's hand in death 27
- Suffering in God's purpose 31
- The death of the faithful 34
- Death and loss of faith 38
- The good life 42
- A good death 47
- Preparation for death 51
- When He calls me 54
- Is death a loss? 57

- Tested for heaven 61
- What will they say about me? 64
- What will God say about me? 68
- Accuse yourself before the
  accuser does 71
- Remember 75
- Do not judge the dead 78
- When God saves you from death 82
- We have no permanent abode in
  this world 87
- We are citizens of heaven 90
- And we shall be satisfied 95
- There is rejoicing in heaven 98
- The destiny of the righteous 102
- The joy of heaven 105
- Mourning the dead 109
- Coping with grief 112
- Moving on 118
- Helping those who grieve 123
- Care for the aged and dying 127
- Praying for the dead 133

- Prayers 144
  - Prayer for healing for a sick friend 144
  - Prayer for healing for a sick relative ...145
  - Prayer for the dying 146
  - Prayer for a deceased friend or family member 147
  - Prayer for a good death 149
  - Office of the dead 151
    - ❖ Morning Prayer (LAUDS) 152
    - ❖ Evening Prayer (VESPERS) 163
- Lord, I want eternal life 173

★★★★★

"As the separation of the soul from the body is the death of the body, so the separation of God from the soul is the death of the soul. And this death of the soul is the true death....Thus the violation of God's commandment is the cause of all types of death, both of soul and body, whether in the present life or in that endless chastisement. And death, properly speaking, is this: for the soul to be unharnessed from divine grace and to be yoked to sin. This death, for those who have their wits, is truly dreadful and something to be avoided. This, for those who think aright, is more terrible than the chastisement of Gehenna. From this let us also flee with all our might. Let us cast away, let us reject all things, bid farewell to all things: to all relationships, actions and intentions that drag us downward, separate us from God and produce such death. He who is frightened of this death and has preserved himself from it will not be alarmed by the oncoming death of the body, for in him the true life dwells, and bodily death, so far from taking true life away, renders it inalienable."

St. Gregory Palamas

If we were required to die twice, we could jettison one death.

But man dies once only, and upon this death depends his eternity.

St. John Vianney

11 Unforgettable Quotes from Saints on Death and Purgatory
Published by Theresa Zoe Williams

Epicpew.com

GONE BEFORE US…

LIFE IS A GIFT

¹⁰For we are what He has made us, created in Christ Jesus for good works, which God prepared beforehand to be our way of life.

Ephesians 2:10

To exist is a privilege. None of us merits existence; God ordained that we are born out of countless options. He willed us into existence because He has a purpose for us. Our essence precedes our existence. We are alive because God has a purpose. We are not in existence to create a purpose for ourselves.

The life we have is a gift from God to us and how we live it is our gift to God. God has given us life and He wants us to serve, honour and glorify Him with it. He wants to rejoice over us. The Lord also wants us to use our lives to bless other people. He wants people who meet us to thank Him for sending us their way.

When a person dies, two dates are written – the day the person was born and the day the person died. In between those dates is a dash. For instance, we could have Emmanuel Gukena (1905-1970). In between the two dates, there is a dash. That dash is the most important part. That dash tells the story of the person – how they have lived, their entire life journey. That dash tells whether they are a blessing or if they just existed. What is your own dash? What happens in your dash? What stories will it tell?

Let us use our dash to make a difference in the world. The Lord has invested so much in us so that we cannot just pass through life without making a difference, without blessing others significantly, without making our existence count, without bringing joy and hope to others.

We cannot allow our existence to be insignificant. We cannot afford to let God down. We cannot afford to live a wasted life, a life that doesn't acknowledge the Maker, a life not driven by vision, purpose and values. A life of self-indulgence, self-centredness and licentiousness is life being wasted.

Life is like a loan. We cannot afford to spend it carelessly. We must trade with it, make a profit and return it to the giver with interest. The Bible says to Him who has, more will be added. Those who make good use of the gift of life, will receive something better. They will receive eternal life.

Let us cherish our lives, spend our time well and carefully, judiciously and fruitfully, so that when we have to return it to the giver and render an account of how we have spent it, our dash will receive commendation and praise and not condemnation and blame.

PRAYER
Lord Jesus, thank you for the gift of life. Help me to cherish this gift, to honour you with it, to bear fruit and to be a blessing to others. When I return to you what I have received on loan, may I return it with great interest and be worthy of eternal life. Amen.

★★★★★

LIVING IN THE NOW

Do not remember the former things or consider the things of old. ^{19} I am about to do a new thing; now it springs forth, do you not perceive it? I will make a way in the wilderness and rivers in the desert.

Isaiah 43:18-19

Many people are existing but they are not living. Many people are alive but simply wasting away their existence. Many are missing the wonder and the joy of life. So many people have chosen to spend their lives in misery, in hatred, self-pity and bitterness, in constant worry and dissatisfaction. All of these are enemies of a good life.

The beauty of life is being able to see the wonder of the moment. Many of us are tied to the past, always looking back, unable to see what is happening in the now. We are tied to the problems of our past, our past mistakes, our past faults, what someone did to us in the past. We cannot move beyond the hurts and disappointments of the past. We refuse to experience new life and be free and instead we keep blaming people. We blame our present on our past.

Many are also always seeking something - pursuing a dream, chasing an ambition, always anxious about what may be. Some people are experts in worrying about the future. They are always worrying and if there is nothing to worry about, they concoct a problem and they start worrying about it. In this way, they never sit back, relax and enjoy the present.

Sadly, we cannot change the past, it is lived and fixed. We don't have so much control over the future because it is beyond our purview, but if we make the best of now, we can atone or compensate for the past and guarantee a promising future.

There are so many opportunities, blessings, wonders, beauty in the now. There is enough to be grateful to God for in the now. Many people will live in the past till they die and many only look to the future which they will never get to live in because the future is always elusive. Tomorrow will always remain tomorrow, while the past is fixed. The future is evasive.

Living in the moment doesn't mean we forget the past or fail to plan for the future. It doesn't mean some self-deception about now because sometimes now can be tricky, lonely, sad or tragic. However, living in the now means realising what we have control over and seeking to make the best of it, instead of lamenting over what we can't change or basing our happiness on what is not ours and what we can't be sure of.

Let us learn to live in the now. Let us celebrate what we have now. Let us be grateful for what we have now. Let us enjoy our now. Let us come out of the past, worry less about the future and just consider the good and beautiful things that God has given us to enjoy now.

PRAYER

Lord Jesus, I am sorry for any way I must have failed you in my past. Forgive me and help me to move on. I surrender my future to you. I refuse to worry about it and I choose to trust and open my eyes to see what you are doing for me now. Help me to be grateful and to make the best use of the opportunities you are providing for me now.
Amen.

LESSONS FROM THE GRAVE

Who can live and never see death? Who can escape the power of Sheol?

Psalm 89:48

I know many people are very afraid of the cemetery. People do not like going around the cemetery or even seeing a picture of one. They find the whole imagery, the environment, the climate very distressing. Interestingly, the gravesite is a place where we can learn a lot. In fact, there are three places where I often learn sober but powerful truths.

- **Hospital**: It reminds me of the value of health and how much I need to be grateful to God and to be sensible in taking care of myself.

- **Prison**: Here I learn to reflect on, cherish and appreciate the gift of freedom.

- **Cemetery**: The cemetery is a good school or classroom for the soul. It is a place of the dead where we can learn great lessons about life.

These are some of the lessons I have learnt and continue to learn from the cemetery.

I.   To make the most of my time here on earth because sooner or later, I am coming here.

II. I won't get out of the world alive, I must pass through this place. I am forced to ponder on the inevitability of death.

III. I didn't come to this world with anything and I won't leave with anything. Whatever

I have acquired or worked for, I will leave behind.

IV. I learn humility. The grave is a place of equality, there is no superiority or power tussle. Those things that cause fracas in a human relationship are insignificant after all.

V. I am reminded that I am dust and unto dust, I shall return. What is most important is my soul, the state of my soul. It is what is eternal and I must care more about its eternal destiny.

VI. I am reminded that in the long run, I will be alone. Those I love and I, shall say goodbye to each other. None of them will follow me to the grave at that time. I must not follow the crowd to offend God because, in the long run, it will be me and God and not "us."

VII. I learn that everything in life has an end - joy, sorrow, worries, troubles, success, achievement, titles, position, ambition. Everything will end when I come here.

VIII. I learn that the human person is not as powerful as we seem because even the most powerful on earth cannot rebel against the sentence of the grave.

PRAYER

Lord Jesus, as I contemplate the mystery of death, may I receive strength from your victory over the grave. May I find consolation in the knowledge that when these mortal remains are laid to rest, my soul shall rise again to share in the blessings of the resurrection.

Amen.

THE VALUE OF TIME

*For everything there is a season, and a time for
every matter under heaven*

Ecclesiastes 3:1

Time is one of the greatest gifts that God has given to us. The souls in hell wish they could have extra time to come back and repent and work for their salvation. Sadly, their time is up and no matter the regret, they cannot change their eternal destiny.

Souls in Purgatory wish they could have time to come back to earth, to do penance, to repent, to multiply good deeds, to love God more. Sadly, there is no time for them to do what was left undone.

While on earth, we often waste time, we spend time in idle pursuit, in frivolous affairs. We do not value time.

- Time is invaluable.

- Time lost can never be recovered.

- Time is given to us in measured proportion.

- No one has eternity, we only have time.

- God has allotted time to each of us and has hidden from us the measure that we have.

Some think they have so much time, but they are deluded. Some think they have very little time, but they are wrong. Since we do not know the length of time we have, let us spend our time profitably and carefully. Whatever we need to do for the wellbeing of our soul, let us not procrastinate. Procrastination is the enemy of time. Let us not delay what is necessary for our eternal wellbeing.

- If we need to make a confession, let us not delay it.

- If we need to do penance, let us not waste time.

- If God has planted a good idea, mission, or assignment in our minds, let us not delay executing it.

- If we need to forgive anyone, reconcile, or make peace, let us not delay. Time waits for no one.

- If we need to be kind, generous and helpful to anyone, let us not postpone it because no one knows what will happen in the next minute.

- If we need to appreciate, commend, or encourage anyone, let us do so immediately. Sometimes we delay until the person is no more. We are then left to appreciate the dead instead of doing so when they are living.

- If we need to disclose vital information to someone, let us do it when we can, before we wish we had.

Let us use our time to seek God, to love Him more, to work for Him, to do penance, to bless others, to reconcile, to atone for our sins. Let us use time to prepare for eternity.

Once our time is up, we cannot even add a second. We cannot request for a fraction of a second to sigh or utter a syllable.

One day, our own time shall be up, like those who have gone before us. We shall exit this world and the world shall continue to be without us. Others will continue to use their time until it's up and they too will join us.

Let us not over rejoice or be careless with time. Every second is an infinite gift. All the wealth of a state cannot afford an extra minute when one's time is up - this is how precious time is. Our clocks are ticking, and we are gradually moving to the end, when the clock will stop, and we shall be called from this world. Let us think of this and gain wisdom of heart.

PRAYER
Lord Jesus, help me to spend my time wisely in pursuing eternity. When my time comes to an end, may I be fully prepared to face the road to eternity without reluctance and regret.
Amen.

★★★★★

15

REMEMBER YOU ARE DUST

By the sweat of your face, you shall eat bread until you return to the ground, for out of it you were taken; you are dust, and to dust you shall return.

Genesis 3:19

Every Ash Wednesday, the Church reminds us, through the imposition of ashes on our forehead, that we are dust and unto dust we shall return. This is a sobering but important truth that we need to ponder on every day of our lives here on earth.

This statement that we are dust and to dust we shall return carries a lot of weight and reminds us of a lot of things. Remember you are dust reminds us of our originality, connectivity, frailty, unity, vanity, mortality.

I. Originality:
We are reminded that no matter how beautiful we may be, our original constituent is dust. What we are is smeared on our forehead. We came from dust through an act of God. God is involved in our journey from the beginning.

II. Connectivity:
We are all connected to one another and to nature. We are all dust. I always remind myself of this when I am standing before powerful people and I am feeling tense or nervous. I remind myself that even the people I consider powerful are fundamentally like me. They are dust; we came from the same place.

III. Frailty:
You are dust reminds us that we are weak and frail. Sometimes we expect so much from

ourselves and others also expect too much from us. We must always remind ourselves that we are merely dust. Even God thinks of us as dust and so He has compassion on us. The Psalmist says the Lord has compassion on us just as a father has compassion on his children. He knows what we are made of. He remembers we are dust.

IV. Unity:

We are united with the whole of creation. We are dust living on dust. Together with all creation, we shall return to the earth and so we are a part of the big family with all other creatures. In a sense, we are at home on the earth because we came from it, even though we are not ultimately earthly because of God's Spirit in us. We should therefore respect nature, mother earth and the whole of creation, recognising that we belong one to another and like the whole of creation, our bodies shall return to the same place.

V. Vanity:

No matter how powerful, beautiful, rich, celebrated or decorated we are, we are still dust and unto dust, we shall return. This should teach us humility. When we are tempted to tell people how great and well connected we are, let us remind ourselves that we are merely dust and ashes.

VI. Mortality:

Putting ashes on our forehead is a good way of reminding ourselves what we do not like to think about – our mortality. We are ashes, we are dust and we shall return to dust. We are not to live forever in this world. One day, dust shall return to dust. Let us keep this in mind and gain wisdom that we are not permanent here. Like the Psalmist, let us number our days so that we may gain wisdom of heart.

When we hear that we are dust, we are reminded that this flesh is dust and it shall return to the earth. Our soul is what is immortal in us and so we should not over pamper the flesh at the expense of the soul. Our mortal bodies shall return to the earth, our souls will return to face their Creator. We shall rise again not with this body but with a glorified body. Let us not allow the love of what is material, provisional and fleeting to jeopardise what is ethereal, spiritual, and eternal.

PRAYER:

Lord Jesus, may I keep in mind always that I am dust and one day, dust shall return to dust. When my earthly body returns to where it came from, may my soul never be deprived of your presence. For from you it comes and may it return safely to you.
Amen.

★★★★★

THE FEAR OF DEATH

My heart is in anguish within me, the terrors of death have fallen upon me.

Psalm 55:4

We are all afraid of many things in life - fear is part of life. However, fear is a big problem when it restricts and controls us, when it robs us of the joy of life and the wonder of the moment.

One of the things many of us are so afraid of today is death. Many of us are afraid to even think of dying. We recoil from thinking of our death.

We are afraid of death for mainly three reasons:

- The painful process of dying
- The sadness of leaving behind those we love
- The uncertainty of where we are going.

Dear friends, death is inevitable, a reality we all must accept. Every day we live draws us closer to that reality. Instead of living in fear of it, let us prepare for it. Let us seek to live good lives and let us pray to the Lord to help us overcome the fear of death. Let us also always think of death as a passage to spend eternity with Jesus.

Fear of death kills so many before their death, but the hope and joy of spending eternity with Jesus help us to look beyond fear to hope, beyond darkness to light, beyond gloom to glory.

PRAYER

Lord Jesus, help me by the power of the Holy Spirit, to overcome the fear of death and to await with joyful hope, my eternal fellowship with you in heaven.
Amen.

★★★★★

CATEGORIES OF DEATH

³² But we had to celebrate and be glad, because this brother of yours was dead and is alive again; he was lost and is found.'"

Luke 15:32

Often, when we talk about death we talk about physical death, the separation of the inner being from the outer being, the detachment of the soul from the body. This actually relates to physical death but I will call our attention to other forms of death.

I. Physical death:

This is the separation of the soul from the body. This is when a doctor or a certified medical personnel pronounces a person dead.

II. Spiritual death:

This is when a person separates themselves from God, the source of life and grace. This is caused by sin. This was the death God referred to when He warned Adam and Eve against eating the fruit.

III. Pragmatic death:

This is when a person is alive but living their lives in a way that renders them useless to themselves and to others. When a person lives irresponsibly, carelessly, bringing sadness and pain, sorrow and heartache to those who care for them, such a person could be said to be pragmatically dead. When we do not contribute meaningfully to life by our existence, when our existence doesn't make the lives of anyone better, it is a subtle death.

IV. Social death:

Social death is when one wilfully estranges themselves from family and friends, from people who care for them. It is when one chooses to alienate oneself from the support and love of their natural family or their spiritual family, which is the Church. The father of the prodigal son told the elder brother that his brother was dead but now alive. The father describes the prodigal son's adventure and isolation as a form of death.

Many people have come from a difficult family background and for certain reasons, they have excluded themselves from everyone in their family. We cannot reject our entire family. God didn't make a mistake when He made us come through a particular family. Everyone in our family cannot be evil. Even when God called Abraham, He allowed him to take Lot along. I have had to preside at funerals of people whose family members are unknown and you can see that this person had died even before their death.

V. Eternal death:

This is worse than any kind of death. This is when a soul is denied entry into the presence of God. This is when a soul is sentenced to eternal damnation. The Bible calls this the second or final death. This is worse than physical death and is a death we ought to dread with all our body, mind and soul.

Our souls are made to rest finally in God and if they are deprived of God's presence, they are deprived of eternal life, rest and peace. A soul condemned to an eternity in hell is a soul that is finally dead.

PRAYER

Lord Jesus, you have come so that we may have life and have it to the full. Save me O Lord from death while I am still alive and when my soul is separated from my body at a time you have appointed, may I not be separated from your presence.
Amen.

GOD'S HANDS IN DEATH

Since their days are determined, and the number of their months is known to you, and you have appointed the bounds that they cannot pass,

Job 14:5

Often, when our loved ones pass away, we not only get angry and agitated but we become over-obsessed with analysing the cause of their death.

In many West African cultures, when someone dies, there is always the suspicion that the death must have been caused by evil people. This is especially so when someone dies suddenly, at the prime of their life, after having a misunderstanding, after achieving a giant stride or when anticipating a significant celebration.

In western culture also, when someone dies, there is always the possibility of excessively trying to fathom if the death was caused by a failure in the medical intervention they received.

The consequence of this is that we begin to shift blame. This leaves us very bitter and it makes it more difficult to accept what has happened. Interestingly, after tossing the blame around, we then push everything to God for not intervening in the whole process.

Dear Child of God, let us keep this in mind. It is God who has numbered our days. Nobody dies without His permission. If He allows someone to die, it is because the time allotted for that person has elapsed. No matter how we try, we cannot increase our length of days. Even though people can sometimes act carelessly and in ways that could cost them their lives, no one can cut short his days without God's approval. Nobody comes to the world without His knowledge and approval and no one leaves without it.

Therefore, even when we search for causes, we must always come to the conclusion that if God doesn't allow it, it won't happen and if He allows it, it is because He wills it.

The death of Jesus seemed a great tragedy caused by the animosity and ingratitude of a people. It felt senseless for Jesus to die the way He died, but guess what? It was in God's plan. It happened as God had predetermined. Yes, it was through malice, but the malice was working out a divine purpose.

Nobody can kill another person or preside on the destiny of another except if God allows it and whatever He allows is for a purpose. God will never allow anything that will upset His purpose and designs for us. In the long run, life and death are in the hands of God.

So let us see God's hands in every death, no matter how painful. Let us resign to His will which may not always be intelligible to us but is always good.

PRAYER

Lord Jesus, help me to accept that nothing can happen to me or my loved ones without your knowledge and permission and that because you are infinitely good, you won't permit anything which will contradict your good purpose.
Amen.

★★★★★

SUFFERING IN GOD'S PURPOSE

For though in the sight of others they were punished, their hope is full of immortallity.⁵ Having been disciplined a little, they will receive great good, because God tested them and found them worthy of Himself;⁶ like gold in the furnace He tried them, and like a sacrificial burnt offering He accepted them.⁷ In the time of their visitation they will shine forth and will run like sparks through the stubble.

Wisdom 3:4-7

One of the things that have troubled many of us so much is to see the dying suffering. Sometimes we even pray that God should take someone away because their suffering and pain are too much to bear.

Sometimes we wonder why some people have to suffer so much in life. We get confused all the more if the person suffering is someone we judge as faithful to God.

Dear Child of God, suffering is one of God's means of purifying and perfecting us. Often, God allows the righteous to suffer before death as a means of pruning, cleansing and preparing them for Himself. God in His wisdom and providence allows devout souls to go through some period of suffering as their own purgation here on earth.

God is very loving and merciful, so if He permits anyone to undergo a period of great suffering and pain, it is an act of mercy and not wickedness. Let us pray for insight to see things from God's perspective and not from our own imperfect view.

PRAYER

Lord Jesus, I surrender myself to you, I unite all my suffering with yours. I accept whatever suffering you will for me, provided I will be worthy of your presence.

Amen.

★★★★★

THE DEATH OF THE FAITHFUL

Precious in the sight of the Lord is the death of His faithful ones.

Psalm 116:15

The Psalmist tells us that the death of a faithful soul is precious in the eyes of the Lord. There are two ways to interpret and understand this. The keyword is precious - יָקָר (yā·qār). Yaqar means precious, weighty, expensive, valuable, splendid.

At one level of interpretation, this means that the death of a holy person is something very special to the Lord because it is a homecoming, it is a perfection of fellowship between the Father and His child. When someone departs this world in a state of friendship and faithfulness to God, heaven prepares a great welcome for the person. The angels bear the person. There is a great celebration in heaven, something like a heavenly coronation ceremony, celestial jubilation, a kind of hallowed party.

Just as we are joyful when a new child that has been eagerly awaited comes to a family, in the same way the death of a holy person is their birth day into heaven. God doesn't want the death of a sinner because it means the soul is forever lost from His presence. A divine loss is when a soul dies in a state of sinfulness. A divine gain is when a soul is purified and ready to join the household of God.

A second level of interpretation is that the Lord values the death of His faithful so much. He cares so much about a faithful soul; their death is weighty before God.

In the New Living Translation, it is written: The LORD cares deeply when His loved ones die.

As much as God loves to be reunited with His beloved ones, He doesn't hurry to take His faithful children from this world and when He does, it is because it is absolutely necessary for their wellbeing and salvation. To call His faithful from this world is an important decision for the Lord to make.

This seems to be the sense in which David wrote these words because he wrote them while praising God for delivering him from death.

Therefore, let us keep in mind that the souls of everyone are dear to God. He loves them, He wants His faithful children to come to the joy of His presence, but He doesn't just take them from the world. It is a precious decision, a weighty matter for the Lord. Our feelings and sadness are not unknown to the Lord but then He decides in favour of the eternal wellbeing of His faithful.

PRAYER

Lord Jesus, whenever anyone I love is called from me to your side, help me to know that you have decided what is best for them. May I know the comfort of your Spirit and find hope and light in my grief.
Amen.

DEATH AND THE LOSS OF FAITH

³⁸ For I am convinced that neither death, nor life, nor angels, nor rulers, nor things present, nor things to come, nor powers, ³⁹ nor height, nor depth, nor anything else in all creation, will be able to separate us from the love of God in Christ Jesus our Lord.

Romans 8:38-39

I have met people who told me that they were once believers but they separated themselves from God after the painful loss of someone very dear to them. Many people are very angry with God because of the loss of someone dear to them and sometimes because of the circumstances leading to the death. Some people's anger is fuelled by the fact that they prayed to God to spare their loved ones and yet the person still died. For them, this can only mean that God is heartless or He just doesn't exist and we are actually ruled by unpredictable chance.

When we are in this state of stark pain and anger, we become vulnerable and the devil tries to manipulate our minds by suggesting some faith-destructive thoughts and ideas to us.

Dear friends, we need to keep some things in mind.

I.   Life is a gift from God and He alone determines when we come into existence and when we go.

II. Everyone belongs to God. No matter how close we are to our mum, dad, children, sibling or friend, they belong ultimately to God. It is His will that we know them and enjoy them for a while. But ultimately they belong to Him and so if God calls anyone we love to Himself, He has only called one of His own.

III. No matter how much we love someone, we cannot love that person more than God. God's love is faithful and infinite. He acts towards everyone with this perfect love so if in His love, He calls someone we love, let us learn to surrender to Him who loves them most.

IV. God knows the best for everyone. We may want a long life, good health, wealth and recovery for someone but God knows best. God cares so much about our feelings. He doesn't want to hurt our feelings but our feelings cannot override His purpose. If it is best for God to call someone to a place of rest, our sorrows will not stop Him from doing what is best. We may not understand now but we shall all understand later, praise His wisdom and realise how foolish we have been to have challenged Him.

V. Our praying to God doesn't control God. We need to understand this. Our prayers are not meant to force God to please us, they are meant to help us to see things from God's perspective and accept whatever He wills. So, if we pray for recovery and God calls the person to Himself, it is because God has a plan that is better than our wish. This doesn't mean that our prayers are not necessary or unanswered but that they are answered in God's way. We may want a temporal recovery and God calls the person from the world of sickness to a better place.

It may interest us to know that some of the people we sorrow about and on account of whose death we "hate" God, are thanking God for calling them from this world and if they were to choose, they would never choose to come back to us.

I acknowledge that these facts are sometimes difficult to understand after the painful death of a loved one but then these are the truth that can bring us healing and stability.

PRAYER
Lord Jesus, no matter what happens to me, no matter how broken I am, may I learn resignation to your will and may I never stop praising your wisdom, which is immediately beyond human fathoming.
Amen.

THE GOOD LIFE

¹² I know that there is nothing better for people than to be happy and to do good while they live. ¹³ That each of them may eat and drink and find satisfaction in all their toil—this is the gift of God.

Ecclesiastes 3:12-13

As I write this reflection, I remember the death of a young lady named Princess Emmanuella Mbanogu. I was challenged by the testimonies of people who knew her. Everyone seemed to agree that she was a blessing to others and that she lived a very good life. For many of us, her life was too short but then it was a good life.

What then is a good life?

For some, a good life is a life of pleasure and enjoyment, indulging ourselves and satisfying our base appetites. Many people understand the good life as a life of great riches. To be rich and able to procure anything money can buy is a good life. Many people equate a good life with a long life. Someone who lives to see their third or fourth generation has lived a good life. For some, it is a life free of worries, troubles and pains - a life lived in good health and rest of mind.

The topic of a good life is also a question of philosophical debate.

The Sophists said it is a life of knowledge but then no one can know anything with certainty. Aristotle said a good life is a happy life, a fulfilled life. This is achieved through virtues, through character, good reasoning and good relationships with others. For him, a good life gives pleasure but a life of pleasure doesn't mean a good life.

For Socrates, a good life is not in wealth nor in material acquisition. It is a life of love, truth and virtue.

For me, a good life consists in the following:

I. Happiness and contentment:
It is not in a life of self-pity, guilt, hatred, feeling we are worthless, that we are not good enough, focusing on what we do not have, counting other people's blessings, regretting the past, blaming others, feeling bitterness and wasting our energy in sorrowful living.

A good life consists in loving, accepting and being happy with oneself. It is the understanding that we are not perfect, so therefore we need to improve in certain areas of life yet without judging, condemning, hating or beating oneself up.

II. Good relationship with family:
A family is an oasis of support. We may not have come from the best family but estranging ourselves from our family is not a good way to live.

III. A life of inspiration and blessing:

A good life is a life that inspires others, that others can learn from. It is a life that touches and challenges others, an exemplary life that people can emulate.

IV. It is a life of integrity:

A good life is a life in which one doesn't tarnish their integrity, in which one maintains their integrity and a good name. It is a life in which one avoids anything that can earn them disgrace, shame or dishonour. It is the opposite of a shameless life.

V. It is a Godly life:

One may be kind and loving but without knowing God, such a life cannot be described as a good life. To know and acknowledge God is at the heart of a good life. To deny the existence of God is what the Bible calls spiritual foolishness and one who is spiritually foolish may live an influential life but it will always fall short of a good life. A life without God is a life of pathetic spiritual poverty. There is no greater poverty than life without faith.

It is impossible to die a good and holy death without living a good life.

PRAYER

Lord Jesus, help me to live a good and godly life. Help me to spread love wherever I find myself, to sow kindness, good examples, godliness and to bear fruits that will outlast me on earth.
Amen.

A GOOD DEATH

Call no one happy before his death; by how he ends, a person becomes known.

Sirach 11:28

A good death is something we all need to pray and prepare for. How a person dies is more important than how they lived, however, how a person lives will largely determine how they will die.

What actually is a good death?

Many people think of a good death as dying peacefully in one's sleep. Some see a good death as dying in the presence of one's family, friends and loved ones. A good death to some is to die without suffering, without pain, without prolonged illness. A good death is to die with a sense of accomplishment and achievement. A good death is to have a very elaborate, breath-taking and expensive funeral ceremony, characterised by an expensive casket, a special gravesite or tomb, with memorabilia to keep the person in memory, and perhaps with halls, streets, schools, hospitals or other public and private properties named after the deceased.

These are good ways of dying but they are not essential in the definition of a good death. A good death is simply a holy death - to die in the state of grace, in a state of friendship with Jesus, to die at peace with the Lord.

When we are at peace with the Lord when death comes, it doesn't matter how we die, whether it be through a car crash, plane crash, through drowning, torture, murder, through spiritual or physical attack, through years of painful sickness and wearing out because of terminal illness, whether we die by fire accident or by any means that the world terms ignominious.

Many of the Saints and martyrs died this way and many Saints in our days will also die this way. But what is most important is not the manner of death but the state of our souls when we die and our relationship with Jesus when we die.

We may not die with family and friends around us but when we die in the state of grace, angels and Saints are around us to comfort us and lead us to heaven. We may die slowly and in pain due to sickness, but the Blood of Jesus purifies us and makes us heaven ready.

We may not have the privilege of a grand funeral, but we shall not be denied the joy of an imperial ceremony in heaven. The rich man in Jesus' parable had a first-class funeral whereas he was thirsty on the other side. Lazarus' body was discarded but his soul was honoured by angels and he enjoyed peace and bliss in the bosom of Abraham. His latter state was better than the rich man.

When we are in a state of friendship with Jesus, death is deprived of its sting. We do not have to battle with it, we welcome it joyfully. We surrender to it with hope and eagerness, knowing full well that it will bring us rest from our earthly labours.

PRAYER

Lord Jesus, I pray for a holy and a happy death. Help me to cooperate with you in life and receive consolation from you in the hour of my death. Amen.

PREPARATION FOR DEATH

*Therefore, you also must be ready, for the Son of
Man is coming at an unexpected hour.*

Matthew 24:44

In life, we are always preparing for something.
We prepare for celebrations, for exams or
tests, for an interview, for a journey, for a
presentation, for an occasion.

Sadly, most people fail to prepare for the most
important thing, which is death.

Ironically, I have met many people who have prepared adequately for their funeral by writing their wills, arranging funeral programs and contacting funeral directors, booking caskets and so on without preparing for death itself. This is the same foolishness of those who prepare for their wedding without preparing for marriage.

Many do not like to think of death but since it is inevitable, it is something we must always prepare for. The worst tragedy in life is to die without being ready or prepared. Since we do not know when death shall come, we must always be ready.

How do I prepare for death?

I.   By keeping it in mind and living each day as if it would be our last.

II. By regular confession and not allowing any hidden sin in our lives. I usually recommend to people, the practice of a lifetime confession, where they will bring the sins of their whole life before the cleansing blood of the Lamb.

III. By doing regular penance and atoning for the temporal punishments due for our sins after

52

the guilt has been removed through confession.

IV. By seeking peace with those we may have fallen out with. The Bible says we must seek peace with everyone and seek holiness, without which no one can see God.

V. By living a good life - a life of peace, charity and love, a life fruitful in good deeds. The Bible says charity saves from death - eternal death of course.

VI. By making friends with the saints in heaven and constantly praying for souls in Purgatory, so that when they are in heaven, they can in turn help us.

VII. By always praying for a happy death and asking for the prayers of St. Joseph, the patron of the dying.

PRAYER

Lord Jesus, help me to prepare for the inevitable. When my sojourn here comes to an end on that day known to you alone, may I not be like the foolish virgins who were not yet ready.
Amen.

★★★★★

WHEN HE CALLS ME

⁸Then the man and his wife heard the sound of the Lord God as He was walking in the garden in the cool of the day, and they hid from the Lord God among the trees of the garden. ⁹But the Lord God called to the man, "Where are you?"

¹⁰He answered, "I heard you in the garden, and I was afraid because I was naked; so, I hid."

Genesis 3:8-10

Some time ago, the news went viral about a popular preacher who had a heart attack and died in a hotel room with a side chick. It was very shameful news, an embarrassing legacy to leave behind and a sad way to end one's life. Each time I reflect on this, I ask myself one question. When He calls me, where will I be? When death comes, where will He find me?

Some people will die when they are fighting for what is useless and vain. Some people will die while committing atrocities. Some will die while seeking illicit pleasures. Some will die whilst pursuing what God has not deigned to give them. Some people will meet death on the way to carry out an evil assignment and some will be embraced by death because of their greed.

Where will death find me?
What will I be doing?
What will I tell Jesus when He calls me?

When Jesus calls me, will I answer, "here I am Lord, I am doing what you sent me, I am working for you, I am in the place you sent me, I am living the life you have called me to, I am still faithful to the assignment you gave me. I am here Lord, ready to give an account."

I love to end with this song which always ministers to me:

When He calls me, I will answer,
when He calls me, I will answer,
when He calls me, I will answer,
I will be somewhere working for the Lord.

PRAYER

Lord Jesus, I pray that nothing will distract me from my service to you. May death not meet me carrying out what you have not sent me to do. When you call me to come from this world, may I be like the servant that the master finds ready when He returns.
Amen.

IS DEATH A LOSS?

For to me, living is Christ and dying is gain.
Philippians 1:21

When someone dies, we call it a loss. We say we have lost them. Is death actually a loss?

St. Paul made a very bold statement - that for Him life is Christ and death is gain. Is death a loss or a gain?

Well, death can be either. It depends on the state of the deceased. For all who sleep in Christ, death is a very great gain. Let us begin to look at why death is considered a loss.

- The person loses his body

- The person is separated from family and loved ones

- We won't see them again

- The person leaves behind everything he/she has worked hard for

- Life with all its promises, dreams, ambitions, and hopes comes to an end.

Let us now address all these. For those who die in Christ, death brings to them something better than life can afford.

- They drop a mortal body in the soil and receive a glorified body.

- We may be separated from our family members on earth, but we are going to a better family.

- Death doesn't mean we won't see our loved ones again. It only means we won't see them for a while. The separation is temporal. We shall be united with those who also died in a state of friendship with Jesus. In heaven, we celebrate our union with those we know but we do not regret those who are damned. Yes, because in heaven there is no regret or sorrow; nothing can cause sorrow for those who are in heaven.

- The deceased may leave behind people they love and things they cherish but who and what they are going to meet is better than what they have left behind. What we have in this world is utterly insignificant and inconsequential compared to what and who we are going to meet.

- Death is not the end of life; it is the beginning of life. In fact, when we die, we pass from the world of the dying to the world of the living.

Death is therefore not a loss for those who die in Christ; it is the greatest gain. The secret of gaining from death is living for Christ. For those who live in and for Christ, death will be for them the greatest blessing, the passage to life everlasting, the door to paradise, the bridge to bliss, the road to glory, the access code to the kingdom of heaven, the final baptism which will bring them into the new Jerusalem with a street of gold.

Death is also a great gain for the family and friends of the deceased because it means they have an intercessor in heaven, they have an advocate before Jesus, they have someone in the highest place who can help them with prayers.

PRAYER

Lord Jesus, may I live wholly for Jesus, may I die in you and may my death be the greatest gain for me and those whom I will leave behind.
Amen.

★★★★★

TESTED FOR HEAVEN

Therefore, my beloved, just as you have always obeyed me, not only in my presence, but much more now in my absence, work out your own salvation with fear and trembling.

Philippians 2:12

Heaven is our homeland. Jesus has gone to prepare a place for us. Heaven is as we described it - a state of eternal happiness with God and all His Saints.

Jesus has paid for us the price of heaven. No one can enter heaven if not for the redemptive sacrifice of Jesus. He has done what we cannot do, however, we must also do our own bit. We have a part to play, a battle to fight, a price to pay too.

Heaven is not a bonanza; it is the greatest reward of all who love God. The joy of heaven is more than the best that the world has to offer. Hence, God demands some things from us before we can come to the joy of heaven.

I. We must prove that we love God above any person or thing. We must pass this test of love. Heaven is for those who love God above all else.

II. We must desire heaven above every other thing and nothing in this world must appeal to us more than heaven.

III. We must overcome the temptations of the devil who will do everything to steal our eternal inheritance.

IV. We must persevere to the end. Many started on the narrow road and fell by the wayside. Many will give up their faith and backslide, but as for us, we must not be like those who look back and lost it. We must press on, fight to the end. Past righteousness has no value before God; it is who we are now that matters.

V. We must hate sin and reject all that God despises. The eyes of the Lord are too pure; they cannot behold any iniquity. Nothing unclean will enter heaven. We cannot be comfortable in sin and entertain the hope of heaven. We either allow the desire for heaven to keep us away from sin or sin will keep us away from possessing heaven.

Let us therefore with fear and trembling work out our salvation. The joys of heaven are worth any sacrifice we could ever have to make here on earth.

PRAYER

Lord Jesus, thank you for paying the ultimate price of heaven for me. Help me to seek first the kingdom of God and to seek nothing more than I seek this. May I be resolved to faithfully follow Jesus who is the way to heaven.
Amen.

WHAT WILL THEY SAY ABOUT ME?

⁴By faith Abel offered to God a more acceptable sacrifice than Cain's. Through this he received approval as righteous, God Himself giving approval to his gifts; he died, but through his faith he still speaks.

Hebrews 11:4

It was by faith that Abel brought a more acceptable offering to God than Cain did. Abel's offering gave evidence that he was a righteous man, and God showed His approval of his gifts. Although Abel is long dead, he still speaks to us by his example of faith.

Quite often, we have heard the question "What will they say about me?" at a funeral but sadly, we don't take it to heart. It is sometimes the case that we take to heart things that are not very important and push aside important things.

The death of someone we love should always be enough of a sermon for us. When someone dies, everyone comments on who they were, their legacy, their character, their excellence. Often during the funeral, people tend to focus on and testify to the good qualities of the deceased but sooner rather than later, people move beyond the respectful to the truthful. They will say what they really know about the deceased. They will move beyond the patronage of funeral to the reality of who the deceased was. Information hitherto unknown is uncovered, secrets are revealed, news flies, truth is exposed.

Let us pause for a moment and reflect.

- What legacy will I be living behind?
- What will I be remembered for?

- Is there anything in my life I need to address and repair, things that will scandalise people if it is uncovered after my death?

Some people will be remembered for their interest in sport, their love of fashion, their makeup, their love for food and a particular kind of drink. Some will be remembered for their temper and the difficulty in relating with them.
Many will be remembered as troublemakers, husband snatchers, as being vexatious, proud, belligerent, unkind in words and some for how they frustrated others.

What will you be remembered for?

Like Abel, when we die, we still speak. Our examples still speak to people. People's memories of us are our words. As children of God, we must be known and remembered for these things when we leave this temporal world:

- Our faith and our love for God. These can never be hidden.

- Our love and service to others.

- Lives and souls that we have impacted and touched positively. People we have helped not just in material terms but also spiritually.

- We must be remembered for having a Christlike character- love, humility, peace-loving, generosity, sincerity, selflessness etc.

- Our contribution for the growth, peace and unity of the Church, our family, our community, place of work, our association, group, team and wherever we are known.

PRAYER

Lord Jesus, help me to live in a way that means I may leave a good legacy - a legacy which will inspire others to lead good lives. When I am alive, may I be a light in the world and when I am gone, may the light of my witness continue to burn bravely among those who have come in contact with me. Amen.

WHAT WILL GOD SAY ABOUT ME?

21 *"Not everyone who says to me, 'Lord, Lord,' will enter the kingdom of heaven, but only the one who does the will of my Father in heaven. *22* On that day many will say to me, 'Lord, Lord, did we not prophesy in your name, and cast out demons in your name, and do many deeds of power in your name?' *23* Then I will declare to them, 'I never knew you; go away from me, you evildoers.'*

Matthew 7:21-23

It is very important to think of what people will say about us. It is a noble decision if we decide to make positive amends in our lives so that we can leave a good legacy and memory. However, there is something more important than what people will say about us. People's testimonies are not necessarily accurate.

Often people do not really know us. They think they do but they do not. Sometimes people are rather polite, and they conform rather than say the truth which will offend others' sensitivities.
The truth is that God is not going to judge us by what people say but by who we truly are.

We may succeed in building our reputation, creating a good name for ourselves, swaying public opinion in our favour, conjuring a good impression about ourselves in people. However, God doesn't judge by public opinion, impression, or appearance.

We must not exhaust ourselves trying to be good in people's sight. We must be concerned about what God will say about us. God is the righteous judge - to Him nothing is hidden, inconclusive and ambiguous. Anyone He declares pure is pure. Anyone He declares good is good. Anyone He declares false and guilty is false and guilty. The

69

Lord knows our truth. He knows those who serve Him and those who do not. He knows those who are faithful and those who are deceitful.

What will He say about us when we stand before Him?

Let us picture ourselves before God. What will He say about us, our character, our relationship with Him and others, our service, our work?

Shall we be able to stand without shame before Him on that day? Will He call us faithful servant or worthless servant? Will He acknowledge us or deny us? Will our assessment be favourable or pitiable?

If we want God to witness to our faithfulness and sincerity in following Him, let us make the decision today by being who we want Him to say we are.

PRAYER

Lord Jesus, lead me to see myself as you see me, to change what offends your holiness and to repent from what can earn me a reproach when I stand before you in judgement.
Amen.

★★★★★

ACCUSE YOURSELF BEFORE THE ACCUSER DOES

Then he showed me Joshua the high priest standing before the angel of the Lord, and Satan standing at his right side to accuse him. ²The Lord said to Satan, "The Lord rebuke you, Satan! The Lord, who has chosen Jerusalem, rebuke you! Is not this man a burning stick snatched from the fire?"

Zechariah 3:1-2

The Bible describes the devil as the accuser of our brethren. The devil keeps records of our mistakes, faults and sins. He keeps records to accuse us before God, to justify his claim that we are unworthy of eternal communion with God, that we are not worthy to be called a child of God.

The devil comes to the bedside of the dying to accuse them, to force them to look at their sins. He brings all sorts of allegations to make us die in regret and despair of hope of salvation.

In order to render him powerless, to destroy his evidence and render his record null and void, we must first accuse ourselves. Whatever we accuse ourselves of before God, this is forgiven and God clears the record. The guilt of a confessed sin is no longer imputed on us.

This is one great importance of the sacrament of Confession. Here in this sacrament, we destroy the agenda of the devil, we ruin his record and cancel all his allegations. The devil is angry when we confess the sins he has recorded against us. This is why the devil is ready to do anything to discourage people from confessing their sins. He knows that once we confess, we obtain mercy and mercy means we are exonerated from his charges.

Every confession is a mini-judgement. We go there to pre-judge our actions. Unlike after death, the judgement in Confession affords us mercy and grace. After our death, it will strictly be an act of justice - we are either condemned or rewarded.

Let us therefore be resolved to put the devil to shame by overcoming our shame, confessing all our sins with all the shame therein, so that we may obtain a clear conscience, clean record, freedom of soul, and so that we may clear ourselves of the shame that the devil wants us to experience when he begins to roll out our sins, one after the other.

PRAYER

Lord Jesus, thank you for your saving Blood which brings me forgiveness and grace. Draw me closer to your bleeding side. Help me to open every wound of sin, to offload every burden of transgression that I carry. Help me to be intolerant of sin and may I never hide any sin from you in the confessional. Open my eyes to know the sins I need to confess and as I approach you through the priest, may I

> receive complete pardon, may I be fully reconciled
> to you and to others and may I frustrate the agenda
> of the enemy of my salvation.
> Amen.

REMEMBER

²⁵ *"But Abraham replied, 'Son, remember that in your lifetime you received your good things, while Lazarus received bad things, but now he is comforted here and you are in agony.*

Luke 16:25

The way we live our lives is like writing a book. It is arranged in different chapters reflective of the many stages we have passed through.

A time comes in our life when we have to look back, when we shall be made to remember things. We shall be made to look back and remember how we have lived, the things we have done, the choices we have made, the places we have visited, the battles we have fought, the projects we have done, the crosses we have carried, our achievements, the legacy we are leaving, the way we have treated people and the things we have endured.

In the parable of the rich man and Lazarus, the rich man was made to remember, to look back, to recall how he had enjoyed without considering or thinking of Lazarus. He was forced to remember what he did not want to remember.

All of us will be made to remember. Some will look back at their lives with laughter, satisfaction and delight. Some will look back with sorrow, sadness and regret. Some will wish they could go back in time to correct what they have done wrong, to undo what they have done badly, to repair what they have damaged, to work more to achieve what they could have achieved but did not.

Let us be careful of the seeds we sow now, of what we do, how we treat others, how we exercise power, how we address issues, how we judge matters. Let us keep in mind that a time will come when we shall be forced to look back.

If we have done anything that could cause us shame, let us confess this now and do penance while we can. Let us intentionally spend our lives creating good memories and doing things that we want to look back at with gratitude, thanksgiving, satisfaction and pleasure.

St. Paul looked back at his life and he was grateful to God. He said he has fought the good fight, he has finished the race, he has poured out his life like a libation. What he now awaits is the crown of righteousness which the righteous judge has prepared for him.

As we live, let us be careful to create memories that we would like to remember when we are dying and to be remembered for when we are gone.

PRAYER

Lord Jesus, help me to cooperate with you as you write a beautiful story with my life. Help me to make choices that I will look back on with joy, gratitude and fulfilment.
Amen.

★★★★★

77

DO NOT JUDGE THE DEAD

⁵Therefore do not pronounce judgment before the time, before the Lord comes, who will bring to light the things now hidden in darkness and will disclose the purposes of the heart. Then each one will receive commendation from God.

1 Corinthians 4:5

One of the tendencies we need to avoid is passing judgement on the deceased. There was a time that the Christian Church was reluctant to bury someone who had committed suicide because she taught that such a heinous crime against life clearly ruled out the hope of salvation. However, the Church now emphasises the incomprehensible mystery of God's love, the power of hope and the fact that only God can truly decide and make a definitive pronouncement on the eternal destiny of a soul.

Who could believe that the thief on the right of Jesus would be in paradise with Him? For many people, he died as a thief and so must go to hell. Many people who were there possibly were not aware of the discussion that took place between him and Jesus at His eleventh hour. The man who was a thief all his life is now among the blessed in heaven. He received forgiveness and shared in the salvific fruit of Christ' suffering and death, just at his dying hour. Left to our judgement, this man would be in the basement of hell.

There are many people who, by our human judgement, we would also suppose would be in heaven, but we are wrong. We judge by our limited understanding. We analyse appearance, we assign value based on impression and this is quite often misleading.

There are some people that we conclude must rot in hell but we may be wrong. God sees what we do not see and knows what we do not know. He alone is the righteous judge. Sometimes, people refrain from praying for a deceased person because they believe this person must be in heaven. We may be wrong; they may need prayers more than we can ever imagine.

There may also be some people that we are pretty sure our prayers can't help because they are candidates of hell but we might be wrong. Seconds before death, some people may experience God's mercy. A lot could happen just before someone's death. There are people whose family members have been praying for their conversion. This may happen even when they are dying. There may be a transaction between them and God which we may not be aware of and which may not even be expressed in a way we can deduce.

This is why our obligation to the dead is to pray for them. We are not to be judges, we are not to speculate who goes where, we are not to preside on the eternal fate of anyone. The ways of God are higher than our ways and so His thought and His mercy are beyond our comprehension.

PRAYER

Lord Jesus, I commend to you the souls of the faithful departed. You alone know their fate and faith, you alone know the weight and merit of their life and work. May you grant to them a judgement of mercy and teach me to refrain from passing premature judgement.
Amen.

WHEN GOD SAVES YOU FROM DEATH

For you have delivered my soul from death, my eyes from tears, my feet from stumbling. ⁹ *I walk before the Lord in the land of the living.* ¹⁰ *I kept my faith, even when I said, "I am greatly afflicted";* ¹¹*I said in my consternation, "Everyone is a liar."*¹² *What shall I return to the Lord for all his bounty to me?* ¹³*I will lift up the cup of salvation and call on the name of the Lord*

Psalm 116:8-13

There are times when we come close to death. There are times when we or our relatives have believed that we wouldn't survive an incident but God showed us mercy and we are back on our feet.

Some of us have survived a life threatening situation, accident, war, sickness, attack, violence, anguish and so on. Some of us have narrowly escaped death. Some people have had a near-death experience. I have read stories of those who had near-death experiences. Some actually died and the Lord brought them back. Many have recounted their experiences. Some were transported to see the reality of life after death - some saw heaven, Purgatory and hell. Some even had a foretaste of what their judgement would have been, but God showed them mercy and resuscitated them.

Some have had experiences where they were unconscious for days and suddenly God restored them. I knew of a person who was resuscitated at the exact time the doctors had concluded with the family members to unplug his life support machine. According to him, he could hear all their conversations, but he just couldn't talk or move. He heard all the prayers said for him, he heard all the poems, songs and words of love said to him by his bedside. He heard it all - his eyes were closed, his body was shutting down but he was conscious in his soul.

Some of us would never have believed that we would still be alive today when we faced the storms of life. We would never have believed that we could survive and still be standing strong, but God showed up for us and here we are today.

The message for us is that we are saved for a purpose. In the Acts of the Apostles, James was arrested and beheaded, Peter was arrested and the angel came to open the prison gate for him to continue his mission. He was saved for a purpose.

Whenever God saves us from danger and death, we must never forget that we were saved for a purpose. We are not saved to a life of sin, indifference and carelessness. I know a man who almost died because of the damaging effect of the excessive intake of alcohol. He was restored miraculously. He was seriously warned to stop drinking alcohol. He obeyed for a while but afterwards went back to the culture of alcoholism and as a result he didn't survive the second health complication he had.

Dear friends, when the Lord saves us from death, He saves us:

I.   To testify to His goodness, mercy and love. We are alive to declare the goodness of the Lord.

II. To give us a second chance to amend our ways and repent of our sins. It is the greatest expression of mercy to be given another opportunity to put our lives in order when we could have spent eternity in suffering if we hadn't been given this chance.

III. God brings us back so that we can strengthen and encourage others by what we have experienced.

IV. God brings us back because He still has an assignment for us. We still have a mission, a purpose, a task to accomplish.

We may not all have this rare opportunity of resuscitation, however, God has given us many chances that are unknown to many of us. He has saved us from many unidentified and unseen evils. He has rescued our lives from the grave, even whilst we were unaware.

We must therefore live our lives in gratitude to God, with utmost care and sense of purpose, with fear of blowing our chance to be saved and as people who are determined never to lose their souls.

PRAYER

Lord Jesus, thank you for caring for me and for your interest in the salvation of my soul. Help me to cherish the opportunities you have given me for my salvation. Help me to be grateful for your mercy and deliverance from death. May I not take your mercy for granted and may I utilise all the provisions you have made for my salvation.
Amen.

★★★★★

WE HAVE NO PERMANENT ABODE IN THIS WORLD

¹⁴ For here we have no lasting city, but we are looking for the city that is to come.

Hebrews 13:14

Often, we tend to forget our status in this world. We are like someone who applied to visit a foreign country and when it was time to leave, he did not want to return.

We have no lasting city in this world. We are visitors, passers-by in this world. What Jesus has promised us is not in this world. If He promised us anything in this world with certainty, it is the fact that we shall face many troubles, difficulties and challenges but in the midst of these, our eyes must be focused on heaven.

We are not to set our hearts and minds so much on the things of this world. We are to store up treasures for ourselves in heaven. Whilst in this world, we are called to do our best to make our lives a blessing to others and to make this world a better place. However, we must never lose sight of the fact that our stay here is temporal, our joy is short-lived and so are our sorrows.

No matter what happens in this world, it is not all that we have. If the whole world was destroyed today, our whole world is not destroyed because this world is not all that we hope for. We have another home in view. Jesus has gone to prepare a place for us.

Whatever we acquire in this world, we shall leave in this world, be it titles, wealth, possession, fame, recognition, properties, power. The things we cherish in this life will not go with us when we leave. We shall kiss goodbye to everything we now cherish as if our joy and life depended on them.

The only permanent place is in heaven. There we shall spend our eternity. What will gain us entrance is holiness, our total love of God and genuine love of others, our good deeds, our faithfulness in trials, the purity of our souls, our decision to prioritise heaven above all the passing pleasures and attractions of the world.

Let us always live in this world not as its permanent members but as sojourners. Let us always keep in mind that heaven is our home and that soon we shall abandon the things of this world in the world and go back home.

PRAYER
Lord Jesus, may I not be lost in the world and lose sight of my true home. Help me to always understand that I am a passing guest in this world and teach me to bring heaven closer to myself and others, even if at least for now, through my meditation and longing.
Amen.

★★★★★

WE ARE CITIZENS OF HEAVEN

But our citizenship is in heaven, and it is from there that we are expecting a Saviour, the Lord Jesus Christ.

Philippians 3:20

A friend of mine rang me recently and he was so excited on the phone. He was so happy because he had been given his citizenship in the United Kingdom. It's a great thing, isn't it?

St. Paul tells us in our text that for us, our citizenship is in heaven. Another translation says, "our homeland is in heaven."

Let us reflect on what it means to be citizens of heaven.

While on earth we value our citizenship and all the benefits it confers, especially when we are citizens of a developed country. Let us be reminded that as Christians, we have the most exalted citizenship - we are citizens of heaven, with all the rights and privileges. We are resident aliens on earth.

This implies at least five things

I. *Our conduct and character on earth must match our citizenship.*

As fellow citizens with the Saints in heaven, we must live and behave accordingly. St. Paul tells us not to conform to the pattern of this world but be transformed by the renewing of our minds.

Jesus reminds us that we are in the world but not of the world. We must practise and celebrate our heavenly culture of holiness, even in this foreign land.

II. Our love should flame towards heaven and we must feel attached to it.

Heaven is our homeland and we should think of it with joy. Our homeland is better than where we are. We should not be afraid or unwilling to return to it when we need to.

In the same way that soldiers in war are always thinking and desirous to return to their homeland, so we should be willing, ready, joyful to think of our return to our true homeland.

III. Even though geographically we are under the government of this world, ultimately, we are under the government of heaven.

Our utmost allegiance must be to the kingdom of God. No matter how bad things are in this world, we have a consolation that this world is not our own. This world is not all we have to rely on, it is not our absolute.

IV. Because we are citizens of heaven, we enjoy certain honours, rights, privileges and benefits that heaven confers on its citizens.

If you are not a citizen of a particular country, you may not be able to access some significant benefits and rights that a citizen enjoys. As a citizen of heaven on earth, you have access to the privileges, rights and benefits that heaven confers on her citizens.

The government of heaven cares about its citizens who are away from their homeland. Heaven cares about you. What a huge blessing. Heaven cares about me. I am important because I am a citizen of heaven residing on earth.

V. Because we are citizens of heaven, we should focus more on building our treasures in heaven.

This is where we shall live eternally. Our stay here on earth is temporal and short. The author of the Letter to the Hebrews tells us that here we have no lasting city, but we seek the city that is to come.

The Lord wants us to prepare ahead for when we shall return to our homeland. While on earth, He wants us to build up treasures for ourselves in heaven, where we shall spend our eternity.

Am I building treasures for myself in heaven? When it is time to depart from this land of my sojourn, will I have made enough preparation for where I am going?

Yes, Jesus has gone to prepare a place for me, but have I prepared myself for the place?

PRAYER

Lord Jesus, help me to remember always that I am a sojourner here on earth and that my real homeland is in heaven. May the consciousness of this pervade my life, choices and conduct in this world. May I one day enter with joy into my lasting homeland in the kingdom of heaven.
Amen.

★★★★★

AND WE SHALL BE SATISFIED

Philip said to him, "Lord, show us the Father, and we will be satisfied."

John 14:8

J esus was talking so freely about God, about the way, about His unity with the Father. Philip interrupted the discourse by asking Jesus to show them the Father and they would be satisfied.

In this statement, I sense a powerful message. Even though Philip uttered this because he had not yet grasped the unity of the Father with the Son, his request should always be our desire - "show us the Father and this will be enough."

Nothing in this world can and should satisfy a child of God. All the attractions of this world must never satisfy us. We must never be too pleased, comfortable and relaxed in this world. The world may offer us pleasure, possessions, wealth, position, power, fame, recognition but these must never satisfy us. This must never be a replacement for our longing to be with the Father.

The best of this world must never be a substitute for the least of heaven.

Only one thing should and can actually satisfy us - that is, to see the Father. This will be enough for us. Once we see the Father, we shall want no more. Human wants are insatiable only in this world. Human want shall be satisfied when we see the Father. We shall want nothing more; we shall seek nothing more. To see the Father is the greatest, the noblest and the biggest ambition. Let us be ambitious for the greatest and let nothing short of it be enough for us.

PRAYER

Lord Jesus, to see the Father face to face is my greatest desire. Help me by the power of the Holy Spirit to live in such a way that my glorified eyes shall one day behold the Father in His glorious light and eternal beauty.

Amen

THERE IS REJOICING IN HEAVEN

After this I looked, and there was a great multitude that no one could count, from every nation, from all tribes and peoples and languages, standing before the throne and before the Lamb, robed in white, with palm branches in their hands. *10* They cried out in a loud voice, saying, "Salvation belongs to our God who is seated on the throne, and to the Lamb!"

11 And all the angels stood around the throne and around the elders and the four living creatures, *and they fell on their faces before the throne and worshiped God, ¹²singing,*

Revelation 7:9-12

Heaven is a place of great joy. Heaven is a place of sweet worship and delight, a place of light and knowledge, a glorious reunion, tranquillity, peace, and satisfaction. It is a place of continuous feast, celebration, and joy.

What do they celebrate in heaven?

The Saints and angels celebrate the greatness, love, beauty, goodness, power, knowledge, justice, and sovereignty of God. They celebrate the wonder of God which is now visible to them. They celebrate their dignity and glory as children of God and members of His household. They celebrate their victory over the ancient serpent, the accuser, over Satan. They celebrate their triumph and the grace of God.

The Saints and angels celebrate their reward which is incomparably greater than their labour. They celebrate the sacrifice of the Lamb, the saving work of Jesus, which is the cause of their own glory, triumph, and honour. In heaven, they fully understand the meaning, eternal effect and purpose of Christ' sacrifice.

They celebrate all the blessings, favours, spiritual blessings and support they received from God, most of which we do not even recognise on earth. They thank God for the suffering which was meant to prune them and prepare them for glory, even though it was very painful while on earth.

They celebrate and rejoice over a repentant sinner who turns to God, because such a person changes status from being a reprobate to being an elect. They celebrate the homecoming of a faithful servant, the birth of a holy person into heaven. The family of a deceased in heaven are especially happy when the person is to be received into heaven. It increases their joy and it's a special solemnity for them.

The feast day of a Saint, their remembrance on earth, their death anniversary or their birthday on earth is also celebrated in heaven. When a Saint is honoured or remembered on earth, the person enjoys great delight in heaven.

On the other hand, when someone in hell is being remembered and praised on earth, it increases their sorrow and suffering.

PRAYER

Lord Jesus, give me your grace to fight the good fight, to finish the race and be worthy of a place in heaven, where I may rejoice and praise you with your Saints for aye.
Amen.

★★★★★

THE DESTINY OF THE RIGHTEOUS

But the souls of the righteous are in the hand of God, and no torment will ever touch them. ² In the eyes of the foolish they seemed to have died, and their departure was thought to be a disaster, ³ and their going from us to be their destruction; but they are at peace. ⁴ For though in the sight of others they were punished, their hope is full of immortality. ⁵ Having been disciplined a little, they will receive great good, because God tested them and found them worthy of Himself.

Wisdom 3:1-5

This is a very powerful passage on the destiny of the righteous. The author tells us that the souls of the righteous are in the hand of God. That is, the righteous are with God, they are with their maker, they are in a place where no torment can touch them.

Even though because of our limitation in understanding, we think of their death as a disaster and we are sad because we see them suffer, the Word of the Lord says they are now at peace. Yes, they are now at peace. The whole suffering and pains of this world dissipate within a second when we experience the joy of heaven.

Great will be the reward of the righteous for all they have to endure on earth. Some were martyred, some endured debilitating illnesses, some were very poor, unloved and ill-treated like Lazarus, some seemed abandoned by God, some were murdered, some carried very heavy crosses in life so that people were questioning the mercy and goodness of God when they saw them.

However, they are at peace. The Lord disciplined them a little and now great is their reward. They bore their crosses patiently, trusting in God and remaining faithful to Him. God tested them and found them worthy of Himself. He tried them like gold in the furnace and they proved faithful.

All their pains in this world are now forgotten. The world thought of them as unfortunate, but they are now blessed. They mourned but are now comforted.

Heaven is a place of peace and comfort, a place of reward for those who remain faithful to God through the crosses, trials, and sufferings of this world. It is a place of reward for those who do not allow their fate to destroy their faith.

PRAYER

Lord Jesus, help me to stand firm in my trials. Help me to remain faithful to you to the end. May I one day cast off my thorny crown and heavy cross and receive a golden crown and the palm branches of the triumphant saint.
Amen.

THE JOY OF HEAVEN

And I heard a loud voice from the throne saying, "See, the home of God is among mortals. He will dwell with them; they will be His peoples, and God Himself will be with them; ⁴He will wipe every tear from their eyes. Death will be no more; mourning and crying and pain will be no more, for the first things have passed away."

Revelation 21:3-4

O ften we think about the fear of death, the sufferings of Purgatory, the torments of hell and we forget to enliven our spirit and animate our hope by contemplating the joys of heaven. Heaven is our eternal home, the home Christ has promised us. By His precious blood, He has purchased a place for us in heaven. Our journey here on earth is just to prepare us for that place. Let us pause for a moment and think of the joys of heaven.

When we get to heaven, our tears, pains, worries, sorrows, and troubles shall disappear. It is a place of joy for all eternity. Many of us are not used to living without worrying. In heaven, there will be nothing to worry about. In heaven, our faith will give way to perfect knowledge. Many of us are asking God "why this and why that?" In heaven, we shall have all the answers because we shall know as He knows and the wisdom and goodness of God shall be justified, even though here and now we question it.

When we get to heaven, there shall be a grand reunion. We shall see our loved ones and relatives who have gone before us, and we shall be happy with them. We shall unite with our family in heaven, the members of the household of God, all the angels and saints. We shall see our guardian angel face to face and be in the company of angels. Together with them, we shall praise God unceasingly with the most beautiful songs of praise and thanksgiving.

We shall enjoy the full glory of being children of God. Now we are called children of God, in heaven, we shall know the fullness of the dignity of our identity. We shall receive the crown of glory and receive the royal robe. Our mortal bodies shall be transformed into a glorious body.

In heaven, we shall be completely happy and satisfied. The greatest joy is that we shall behold God face to face. This is the greatest joy of heaven. Our light and momentary afflictions on earth are preparing for us an eternal weight of glory. Like Peter, we shall say "It is good to be here." All those who have been privileged to experience something of the joys of heaven or see the vision, have unanimously testified that it is indescribable. It is not something that anyone should ever miss.

As enticing as these descriptions are, they do not come anywhere close to what God has prepared for us. This is our human attempt to describe the bliss of heaven. St. Paul says that what no eye has seen, what no ear has heard, what no human mind can conceive is what God is preparing for those who love Him. Let us always contemplate the joys of heaven and live as people who prize it above all their joys.

PRAYER

Lord Jesus, help me to keep heaven in mind. Let nothing in this world satisfy me and deprive me of the joy of heaven.
Amen.

★★★★★

MOURNING THE DEAD

But we do not want you to be uninformed, brothers and sisters, about those who have died, so that you may not grieve as others do who have no hope.

1 Thessalonians 4:13

No matter how pious and mature in faith we may be, the death of our loved ones will always shake us. Death is never something we get used to. Each time it occurs, it is always a new blow. As such, it is right and in fact recommended that we grieve. However, St.

Paul tells us not to grieve like those who do not have hope. This means that as Christians, there is a distinctive way of grieving.

We are not hopeless people. We must grieve with sadness and yet with hope, with sorrow but not with defeat. Our loved ones will rise again. Through the resurrection of Jesus, death is not the final statement on life. Our grief is temporal.

Those who died in the state of friendship with Jesus are in a better place. They are happier than us, they are now with the Lord. Their tears will be wiped and they no longer share in our troubles. They are at peace, they are refreshed, they behold the light and beauty of heaven. We shall be reunited with them one day, where death shall no longer separate us.

This is our hope. This is the truth revealed to us by the Lord. Therefore, let us mourn a little because we shall miss those we love and not because they are lost, because they are never lost but have gone back to where they came from.

PRAYER

Lord Jesus, comfort everyone who grieves. Help them to understand that their loved ones who sleep in Christ are alive with Him in the company of the angels and saints in heaven.
Amen.

★★★★★

COPING WITH GRIEF

The Lord is near to the broken hearted and saves the crushed in spirit.

Psalm 34:18

Grief is something we all have to go through at some point in our lives. It is the pain we feel over the loss of something very dear to us. It may be the breakdown of a relationship or something we wish we could achieve but have to accept the fact that we can't. It could be loss of an opportunity or accepting that we can't have something we desire so much.

Here, I want to focus on the pain of the loss of someone we love.

Even though we all cope with grief differently, the nature of grief is the same, even it differs in degree according to different people. When we are grieving, our feelings are all over the place. We experience pain and resentment, and sometimes denial, apathy, withdrawal and anger. Sometimes we are angry with God for taking away someone we love, someone so good. We are angry with society for not being able to save our loved one from death and with ourselves, with everyone. We hate life.

The period of grief can be very trying. I just want to make some recommendations for coping with grief.

I. The first way to deal with grief is faith. Faith gives us the strength to overcome any circumstance, to see God in every situation. We all need to pray for a deeper faith in God. When something tragic happens, it shakes our faith but only faith can keep us standing. Let us pray always for a stronger faith in the Lord, a faith stronger than our challenges.

II. When we grieve, we enter into a moment of battle with the devil. He knows that when we grieve, we are very vulnerable. This is a time when he tries to manipulate our minds, attack our faith and steal from us. It is a time he wants to destroy our relationship with God and rob us of our joy, peace and strength. He suggests so many things to us, "If God loves you, why would He take this person from you?"

The devil knows that if we understand the love of God and His goodness, we can cope with any grief or loss and so he attacks this understanding first because this is the foundation of strength.

Sometimes he attacks our minds with guilt, accusing us that things would have been different if we had done this or that and so we blame ourselves for the death. In this way, we lose our peace and joy in the Lord. He tells us that the Lord is punishing us and that is why we are in this situation. We must debunk the lies of the devil with the truth of the Scripture.

III. We must understand that life is a strange mixture of good and evil, danger and delight, tragedy and triumph. However, for those who love and trust God, all things shall work for their good. It is not that all things are good - some things are terrible but God can bring good out of them.

Job had no way of knowing that his story would become an eternal blessing for future generations of grievers. God brought something good out of his losses.

Many people have received their vocation, inspiration and spiritual transformation in their moment of grief. We may not see what God is doing at the moment, but God often turns grief into glory.

"It is well with my soul" is a popular and powerful hymn for those facing grief, loss or personal tragedy. It was written by a man named Horatio Gates Spafford, when he was dealing with the sadness of the loss of his four daughters Annie, Maggie, Bessie and Tanetta when their ship collided with another in the Mid-Atlantic. Only his wife Anna survived. This event occurred after some other tragic events in his life. Instead of blaming God, he wrote this song of faith, to praise God and confess that it was well with his soul.

Joseph Scriven also wrote his song "What a friend we have in Jesus" after losing his bride-to-be, just a few days before their wedding.

This is the kind of thing that frustrates the devil.

IV. Let us open ourselves up to the Holy Spirit, for Him to comfort us and be willing to receive the grace of God to strengthen us. Sometimes we just close ourselves to all comfort and resist God's offer of grace. God says we won't be tempted beyond our strength and for every trial, He will provide a way out. He says, "His grace is sufficient for us." Sometimes we need to just go on our knees and ask God for His grace, the grace to cope with the sword in our spirit.

V. Time is a great healer, however, time can also set an ambush - for instance, on the anniversary or birthday of the deceased or at some other family events. We may begin to feel very down but then we should know that there is someone with us, who is by our side and understands our grief – there is no truer friend than Jesus. We can surrender our grief to Him and ask Him for help. He is a faithful friend, He can help us to mend.

VI. Even though some of us may not appreciate people coming to help us or encouraging us in our grief, withdrawal and isolation do not really help us to cope with grief. We need at least one or two people to talk to, to express how we feel and to pray with. There are also organisations and groups that can help us cope with the pains of bereavement. The more we share our feelings, write them down, compose songs out of them, pray through them, then the more we are healed.

VII. We can also ask the Blessed Virgin Mary to intercede for us. She knows the sorrow of losing her husband and her Son. Her intercession can give us strength.

PRAYER

Lord Jesus, give me grace and strength and help me to open myself up to the comforter. May I receive strength and consolation in my moment of grief. May all who grieve the absence of their loved ones be comforted by your grace, your Word, your presence and promises.
Amen.

★★★★★

MOVING ON

The Lord said to Samuel, "How long will you grieve over Saul? I have rejected him from being king over Israel. Fill your horn with oil and set out; I will send you to Jesse the Bethlehemite, for I have provided for myself a king among his sons."
1 Samuel 16:1

When Samuel announced to Saul that God had rejected him, Samuel himself went into a prolonged period of mourning. He could see no way forward. He didn't know the next step, what to do, how to move on. Then, the Lord came to him to tell him that he had mourned enough for Saul and that it is was time to move on. The Lord directed him on what to do next.

Sometimes we feel we just cannot move on in life. We don't know what is next, what to do, how to live. We just feel it is over. This is a time that many people battle with thoughts of suicide. We hate life. Many have lost the will to live.

We don't know how to move on and sometimes we don't even want to move on. We feel it is unfair to move on. We just want to sit and mourn, we close ourselves in and we put our entire life on hold.

After the loss of their loved ones, some people have given in to alcohol and drug abuse. Some have withdrawn from Church, friends, associations, clubs, school, studies and support groups. Some have lost their sweetness, their exuberance, their noble qualities and their fascinating charisma. Some have lost the motivation to work, their creative ideas, their enthusiasm and it affects their output in no small measure.

Some have refused to love or to be loved again, living intentionally in the morass of stagnant melancholy.

I have spoken to people whose lives have obviously come to a standstill. They have shut down their existence as a result of the loss of someone very close to them.

Dear friends, our unwillingness to move on doesn't honour the deceased in any way, rather it dishonours their death. It makes it twice as tragic.

It will be the joy of our loved ones to see us moving on, picking ourselves up again. Our recovery is what gives them joy, not our stagnant sorrow.

Let us also not reject those whom God has sent to us to help us in our moment of grief. There are some crosses we cannot bear alone. We need other shoulders so that we can move on. God supplies these helpers but quite often we file our rejection.

The Lord is willing to supply His grace to those who are ready and open to receive it. He can give us the grace to stand up and move on. He can give us beauty for ashes, He can remove our garment of sorrow and clothe us with joy. Why do you say you can't move on when His words say, "you can do all things." Why do you think your life has come to an end when He says, "my grace is sufficient for you?"

Again, we need to be careful of our confession when we are in such a state because our words are weighty, they release power. When we say negative things, we stay negative.

We must understand that there is no permanent relationship in this world. There was a time we were without those we love, then they came along. Then at some point, we shall also be separated from them for a while. No matter how close we are to our parents, friends, co-workers, siblings, some family members, our spouse or fiancé, no relationship in this world is built on the foundation of permanence. Those we love will depart from us. There is nothing we can do about it. When it happens, our lives just need to carry on until we also depart from those we love. It is the unnegotiable condition of life. This we must accept and prepare for.

The only person that must be necessary in our life is God and God must remain necessary no matter who leaves us. Sometimes we make the necessity of God conditional - He is necessary as long as this person remains also. Once the person dies then God dies in our lives along with the person.

PRAYER

Lord Jesus, help me to know that as long as you live, I can face tomorrow. Help me to know that with you, I can pick myself up again and begin to live. Help me to know that the demise of someone I love doesn't mean it is over and you are done with me. When I am completely down Lord, hold my hands and help me to stand and walk again.
Amen.

HELPING THOSE WHO GRIEVE

15 Rejoice with those who rejoice, weep with those who weep.

Romans 12:15

When we hear of the death of a sibling, spouse, parent of our friends or people we know, we immediately offer sympathy through calls, visits and/or messages. After this, we tend to move on and think we have fulfilled all righteousness.

More so, when we receive different news, we forget the other people who are mourning and we focus on the latest situation. Sometimes, when we see those bereaved consoling others, expressing condolences, we conclude that they have been healed, they have moved on, they have dealt with their grief so well.

Sometimes, we overestimate people's faith and strength and we think they may not really need much support from us. They are walking in faith, they pray in tongues, they are into ministry, they support others, they counsel people and so they will be fine.

In most cases we are wrong. Many people may look like they have dealt with their grief but they haven't. Many look like they are strong but are not really. Even the strong have struggles and they need help.

We all have the obligation of being there for people at these times. We are all called to a ministry of presence. A time of grief is a time when people need our help so much. They need our presence, love, assurance, fervent prayers, intercession, intervention and assistance in doing things. Sometimes people even need our financial assistance to sort things out.

It is not enough to give empty promises. Many people promise the bereaved heaven and earth but time shows that their words are finer than them. Some just give a once-and-for-all phone call, card or message.

We ought to constantly check on the bereaved and send them messages that can motivate, encourage and strengthen their faith and hope. We can book Masses for them and organise prayers to comfort them. We need to think of positive ways to make them know we understand that they are healing, that we know what they are going through, that we haven't left them alone.

As I type this, the Lord is bringing to my mind people who have recently lost their loved ones and need my prayers, counsel, reassurance and support, some of whom I must acknowledge I was not there for as much as I should have been. The fact that someone has resumed work or Church doesn't mean that they are now okay.

Just because someone looks good after a loss doesn't mean they are feeling good. It is when we engage people in genuine love and friendship that we sometimes get to know that there are tears behind the makeup, that their frames are weaker than they look, that the shoe still pinches, that they are disintegrating or have disintegrated from within.

Many are still greatly grieving but silently. They need our sensitivity, charity, affection, encouragement, prayers, support and words of comfort. Let us be our brothers' and sisters' keepers.

This is one of the ways we show that we are children of God, members of one family, interrelated to one another. This is one of the practical ways we show true love and witness to the Gospel.

PRAYER

Lord Jesus, grant consolation to those who mourn. Most importantly, use me as a vessel of joy, hope, encouragement, support and charity for those who are broken and are finding it hard to heal and move on. Help me to be present for them and to be able to reassure them that you truly care.
Amen.

★★★★★

126

CARE FOR THE AGED
AND DYING

*Do not speak harshly to an older man, but speak
to him as to a father, to younger men as brothers,*
1 Timothy 5:1, 4, 8

This is a very sensitive issue and one that I can really get passionate talking about. In my various pastoral visits to the elderly, the aged and the dying, I have observed different attitudes to those advanced in age, unwell as a result of age or just bound by terminal or chronic illnesses.

Some sick and aged people enjoy so much love, care and pampering. I see children who sing for their parents, take very good care of them, bathe those who couldn't bathe themselves, feed them, dress them, spend time with them. I know someone who sings and plays the guitar for his demented mother. She doesn't show that she understand or appreciates it but her son won't miss a day without making the effort to entertain her.

On the other hand, many older people are being neglected, abandoned and uncatered for in their old age. Many elderly people are lonely and desiring death because they are having to endure their old age without tangible love, without dignity and a sense of worth, without a remarkable presence of their family. The language of some children of the elderly is "you are free to die when you want to and how you want to. We shall be waiting for a call and the right time to claim our benefits."

Many parents are abandoned in care homes or old people's homes by the children and grandchildren that they have sacrificed their lives for. Many children who are carers to their aged, ill or demented parents are cruel, intolerant, impatient and mean to their very own parents. A lot of abuse that happens to elderly parents is perpetrated by their own children, even in their own homes.

Interestingly, when these people lose their parents, they shed crocodile tears, browse on the internet very beautiful eulogies, compile them and read them with hypocritical soberness.

Caring for the elderly is not just a good thing but a divine obligation. The Word of God says curse be those who despise their parents in their old age. When the Word of God says honour your father and your mother, it is not just a command for teenagers and young children, it is also for adults.

Some people have given the excuse that their parent(s) did not care for them, therefore they don't feel any obligation to care for their parent(s). They might have even caused us much pain and suffering but the Bible doesn't exempt us on these grounds from caring for our parents. Some of us are just simply selfish and ungrateful. We forget the sacrifices of our parents. We see them as burdens and we are not ready to sacrifice our time for those who sacrificed theirs for us. We accuse them of being messy and unhygienic, forgetting what we were like that once and how they joyfully took care of us. We think they are foolish, forgetting how they patiently taught us how to reason. We complain that their medical bills are too high, forgetting how they never held back their savings when we were sick.

Sadly, some of us don't want our children to be around our aged grandparents. We do not realise that children growing up with elders in their home will value the importance of love, patience, relationships, respect and obedience which are fast eroding in our present world.

I acknowledge that sometimes it can be very difficult taking care of the elderly. Sometimes they can be very assertive and demanding, they can try our patience and push us very far, however, we must care for them as a vocation, an apostolate, a service to God. We need to look beyond the person in front of us to see the person to whom ultimately we render service.

We need to also keep in mind that the measure we give to others shall also be given to us. We may not hope to expect something different from how we treat our parents and elders from our children. If we are opportune to care for those who cannot care for themselves, we must do this with love and empathy as a service to God. We must care for others as we want others to care for us and we want to be treated by God.

If we have someone living with us or our parents are in care homes, it is important to care not just for their physical wellbeing but also their emotional and spiritual wellbeing. We should try and inform our priest so that they visit with the Sacrament and join in offering prayers for the person. We must always pray for them, both for mercy and also that they may go to a place of rest when they pass from this world.

It is a grave sin against the fourth commandment, against the ordinance of charity, against morality, to neglect, despise or be cruel to the elderly. It is a sin that can never go unpunished.

Some of us organise big funerals for people we did not care for whilst they were dying. This is sublime foolishness. To care for people in their old age is more important, rewarding, dignifying and commendable than having an expensive and grand funeral.

We do not need to wait for death to celebrate life. We can begin to celebrate people while they are conscious.

> ### PRAYER
>
> *Lord Jesus, I pray for the elderly. Show them your love and care and instil in me a love for the aged and dying. May I keep in mind always that I might live long enough to become like them and the measure I give now will largely determine what I will get back. Send me Lord to those who need love and empower me to dispense your love and joy to them.*
>
> *Amen.*

PRAYING FOR THE DEAD

¹³ the work of each builder will become visible, for the Day will disclose it, because it will be revealed with fire, and the fire will test what sort of work each has done. ¹⁴ If what has been built on the foundation survives, the builder will receive a reward. ¹⁵ If the work is burned up, the builder will suffer loss; the builder will be saved, but only as through fire.

1 Corinthians 3:13-15

A s Catholics, we believe that God's mercy survives the grave. We believe that our prayers and sacrifices can tip the scale for the deceased. When we pray for the dead, who are those we are praying for?

We are not praying for souls in hell, for they are forever doomed, nor for the souls in heaven, for they are forever saved. We are praying for the souls in Purgatory.

These are souls of those who left this world in a state of grace. These souls kept heaven in mind. They laboured so hard for heaven, battled daily with their weaknesses and imperfections, but died without fully paying the debt of the temporal penalty due to sins whose guilt was forgiven before death. They are also those who are not yet able to behold the face of God because of some venial sins which must first be purified.

Scripture is very clear when it says, *But nothing unclean shall enter [heaven]*.

These are the souls in Purgatory.

Put simply, the souls in Purgatory are those who are not so bad as to be unworthy of God and not so pure to be immediately worthy of God.

CONDITIONS OF THESE SOULS

These souls grievously suffer three major pains:

- *Pain of loss*

  They are temporarily deprived of the vision of God, a vision their souls long, gasp, pant and yearn for, like the deer yearns for running streams.

- *Pain of regret*

  For not loving God absolutely and for not doing enough penance, for time wasted here on earth, regret for not doing enough penance.

- *Pain of sense*

  Fire of purification. Saints Thomas Aquinas, Augustine, Robert Bellarmine and Bonaventure all attested that the pains in Purgatory are greater than the worst in this life.

However, St. Catherine of Genoa, who was granted the privilege of visiting Purgatory several times in her mystical experience, affirmed that though their pains are unimagina-

135

ble and incomparable, they experience spiritual consolations because they have hope. They are absolutely sure of their salvation.

WHY DO WE PRAY FOR THEM?

We pray for these souls because they can't pray for themselves. They rely on divine mercy and our own prayers and sacrifices. God grants some of them the privilege of coming to seek prayers from their relatives and those who can help them.

WHY SHOULD I BELIEVE IN PURGATORY?

As Catholics, we are bound to believe this doctrine because the Catholic Church instituted by Christ under the guidance of the Holy Spirit of Truth, in accordance with the Sacred Scripture and Sacred Traditions, in union with the venerable Church Fathers, has taught us that there is a Purgatory and the souls detained there are helped by our prayers, especially by the sacrifice of the Mass.

THE CATECHISM OF THE CHURCH

The Catechism of the Catholic Church teaches in paragraphs 1030-1032 that:

> "All who die in God's grace and friendship, but still imperfectly purified, are indeed

136

assured of their eternal salvation; but after death, they undergo purification, so as to achieve the holiness necessary to enter the joy of heaven."

PURGATORY AS A CONCEPT

THE WORD PURGATORY
The word Purgatory, just like Trinity, Christmas, incarnation, Mass cannot be found in the pages of the Bible. It is just from the Latin word "purgare", which means to purify, to purge something from defilement. Purgatory is a word used to differentiate the state of those eternally damned in hell and those undergoing purification to attain the holiness necessary for heaven. However, in the Bible, there are texts that shed light on the reality of Purgatory.

PROOFS OF PURGATORY: BIBLICAL PERSPECTIVE

- 2 Maccabees 12:39-46 - Sacrifice for the dead
- Matthew 12:32
- Luke 12:58-59

- 1 Corinthians 15:29 - Baptism for the dead.

- 1 Corinthians 3:13-15

- 2 Timothy 1:16-18 - According to many commentaries and biblical historians, Onesiphorus was dead at this time but then Paul still prayed for him.

TRADITION

I. The Catacombs

The inscriptions and art found in the catacombs (ancient burial places) are replete with inscriptions that offer abbreviated prayers known as acclamations for the dead.

II. All the Holy Fathers and councils of the Church taught the doctrine of Purgatory and praying for the dead as a noble practice.

VISIONS AND APPARITIONS

There are countless apparitions/visions of souls in Purgatory.

Some people believe no one has ever seen Purgatory, that there is no evidence for its existence save through Scripture and the teaching of the Church. They're wrong. We have countless pieces of evidence of people who have seen, been to and have been visited by souls in Purgatory.

- Saint Stanislaus Papczynski (1631–1701), the Founder of the Marian Fathers of the Immaculate Conception, on several occasions, had visions of the Holy Souls asking for prayer.

- Saint Faustina Kowalska (1905-1938), the Secretary and Apostle of Divine Mercy, had visions of the Holy Souls in need of prayers on a number of occasions.

If you need more stories or accounts of the apparition of Purgatory, you can read: *Purgatory: Explained by the Lives and Legends of the Saints* by Rev. Fr. F. X. Shouppe S.J.

COMPARATIVE RELIGION
The practice of praying for the dead pre-dates Christianity and it is found in other religious traditions, for instance:

I. Judaism:
In Judaism, it is called "Kaddish" - A prayer is offered for the dead. ("Kaddish" in Wikipedia, en.m.wikipedia.org)

II. Islam
In Islam, all Muslim faithful have an obligation to pray for the deceased.

Ṣalāt al-Janāzah (Arabic: الجنازة صلاة) is the Islamic funeral prayer; a part of the Islamic funeral ritual. The Salat al-Janazah is a collective obligation upon all Muslims. (Ṣalāt al-Janāzah, Wikipedia, en.m.wikipedia.org.)

III. Pre-Christian Roman religion: They offered votive offerings for the gods on behalf of the dead at specified times - the 3rd, 7th and 30th day.

Many other religions and spiritual traditions also have prayers for the dead as part of their liturgy.

PRAYING FOR THE DEAD AND SIMPLE LOGIC

In the long run, every religious tradition who deny Purgatory, even the Christians, pray for the dead, they just do not clearly understand what they do.

When someone dies, we write RIP which means rest in peace. Rest in peace is a prayer for the deceased to rest in peace.

Both Catholics and non-Catholics observe a moment of silence and wish the soul of a deceased eternal rest.

If someone is in heaven, it is useless for us to pray that they rest in peace. If they are in hell, it is vain to wish that they rest in peace because they can't. This prayer is only sensible, rational and logical if they are in a place where our prayers and wishes can still reach them. That place is unnamed by many but we call it Purgatory.

WHAT ARE WE TO DO TO HELP THEM?

- Book and attend Masses for them

- Say the Holy Rosary, Divine Mercy, Stations of the Cross and other prayers for them. You can gain indulgences for them.

- Receive communion worthily and offer the merits for them.

- Works of charity, penance and offer the merits of your suffering for them.

HOW CAN WE AVOID IT OR SHORTEN OUR STAY?

- Rigorous examination of conscience, our thoughts, words and actions.

- Make regular confessions (with contrition and resolution) and do not take mercy for granted.

- Constantly guard our conduct, regulate our passions and desires. Be watchful of our ways.

- Do penance and mortify our flesh: Some of us over-pamper our bodies. We love comfort too much, we can't wake early, we can't fast, we eat too much, love to drink and enjoy, we can't discipline ourselves. All these sacrifices that people can make here on earth, the penance that many recoil from, they will be forced to undergo worse in Purgatory.

- Seek to gain indulgences: By Stations of the Cross, praying for the Pope, First Saturday devotion, etc.

- Practise virtues such as humility, forgiveness, charity, meekness. Control your tongues in words, food and drink, suffer from patience and perseverance and complain less, instead offering your pains, sufferings, inconvenien-ces to God.

- Be watchful in prayer for yourselves and other souls in Purgatory.

CONCLUSION

Let us love the Holy Souls, for then we will remember them. Love will lead to prayer and sacrifice.

Let us love the Holy Souls, for they are our brothers and sisters, all held in the spiritual cleansing ward of Purgatory, working out their scars and wounds until they can, by God's grace, love the way that God loves, live the eternal life of Heaven, and joyfully participate in the communion of saints.

Let us love the Holy Souls, and they will love us in return. Let us pray for the Holy Souls, and we will never find more faithful intercessors. Let us help to relieve their sufferings, and they will work hard on our behalf, now and at the hour of our death.

★★★★★

PRAYERS

Prayer for healing for a sick friend

Lord Jesus,
Just as the friend of the paralytic brought him to you for healing and you restored him to health, I come before you today bringing *(mention name)*.

Your word says Jesus was wounded for our transgressions, He was bruised for our iniquities: the chastisement of our peace was upon Him; and with His stripes we are healed. For the sake of your sorrowful passion, Lord Jesus have mercy upon *(name)*.

Comfort him/her in his/her pain, show mercy to him/her, I entrust him/her to your care O Lord, may your love be upon him/her. Help him/her also to unite his/her suffering with yours on the cross. May my prayers and the prayers offered for him/her bring about significant improvement in his/her condition.

I also place at the foot of your cross, O Lord, all who are sick, may your agony comfort them. Our Mother Mary, you are the health of the sick, intercede for your children, hold them in your arms as you held your Son. Above all Lord, may your will be done, and may all glory be yours now and for all eternity.
Amen.

PRAY: Psalm 107:19-20

★★★★★

Prayer for healing for a sick relative

Almighty and Merciful Father,
I come before you this day to ask for your healing upon all those who are unwell at this time especially *(mention name)*

You are a loving Father who cares for all your children. Visit with your compassion, your child who lies ill, let him/her experience your healing touch. Lord Jesus, by your wounds we have been healed. By the power of your wounds, I ask for healing upon *(name)*

May the blood shed on Calvary drop upon him/her. Let it wash away his/her sin and restore him/her to health, teach him/her to unite his/her pain with that of Jesus on the cross. May the passion of Christ, strengthen and comfort him/her, and above all, teach him/her to accept the will of God with faith and courage.
Amen.

PRAY: Psalm 34:15-20
READ: Jeremiah 17:14

★★★★★

Prayer for the dying

God of all creation, author of all life and goodness,
I place before you all those who are critically ill, all those who are terminally ill and all those who are dying *(especially/ mention name)*.

Lord Jesus, grant them the forgiveness of the sins of their lifetime, and grant them the comfort of your mercy. May your holy angels be around them, drive far away from them all malicious and foul spirits. To those who do not know you, do not allow them to taste of death without tasting of life. You saved a thief on the cross; grant salvation to all the dying, and do not permit the souls of those for whom you suffered and died to be lost for all eternity.

St. Joseph, you are the patron of all the dying. Beg your Son to embrace all the dying with His love and when they eventually bid farewell to this world, may the doors of paradise not be closed against them.
Amen.

PRAY: Psalm 130

★★★★★

Prayer for a deceased friend or family member

Eternal Father,
Your love is beyond our understanding and your mercy is unfathomable. To you I commend the

soul of your son/daughter *(mention name)*, whom it has pleased you to call from this world.

Grant him/her forgiveness of his/her shortcomings; grant him/her a judgement of mercy, and do not let his/her soul be deprived of your presence for all eternity. Welcome him/her to your kingdom of light, peace, and rest.

May our Blessed Mother, the queen of heaven and earth, intercede for *(mention name)*, and for all souls languishing in Purgatory.
Amen.

Eternal rest grant unto him/her O Lord and let perpetual light shine upon him/her. May his/her soul and the souls of all the faithful departed, through the mercy of God, rest in peace.
Amen.

READ: Jonah 2: 2-9

★★★★★

Prayer for a good death

God our loving and merciful Father, I thank you for the gift of my life and the many ways you have shown me that you are a loving Father, slow to anger and rich in graciousness. I come before you today as your child. I am grateful for the life you have given me and for your sustenance and grace. I acknowledge that my life is a gift from you and that you have fixed the number of my days. I am mindful that I am dust and unto dust this mortal body shall return.

I humbly beseech you that when my journey here on earth comes to an end, may I see Jesus before I see death. Prepare me for the hour of my death and may I never die unprepared. Help me to spend my time wisely, doing penance, making peace, atoning for my sins, and settling my account with you. May my death never be a loss or a painful exit. Silence the accuser, let nothing of him be found with me. May our blessed mother, my guardian angel, my patron Saints, and the holy angels be at my side to console me at the hour of my death.

Holy Spirit, help me to live a good, meaningful, fruitful, and exemplary life and may my life be

149

crowned by a holy death, through Jesus Christ our Lord.
Amen.

St. Joseph, patron of the dying:
Pray for me.

★★★★★

OFFICE OF THE DEAD

Office of the dead is a powerful prayer that the Church says for our departed ones. We are encouraged to pray this for our deceased relatives and friends and for souls in Purgatory generally. It is taken from the Liturgy of the Hours. It comprises an introduction, hymn, Psalms, canticles, Scripture reading, responsory, the song of Zechariah ((Benedictus) if said in the morning) or song of Mary ((Magnificat) if said in the evening), general intercession, concluding prayer and blessing.

MORNING PRAYER (LAUDS)

INTRODUCTION
O God, come to my aid.
O Lord, make haste to help me.
Glory be to the Father, and to the Son, and to the
Holy Spirit.
As it was in the beginning, is now, and ever shall be,
world without end. Amen. (Alleluia.)

HYMN
Jerusalem, my happy home,
when shall I come to thee?
When shall my sorrows have an end?
Thy joys, when shall I see?

O happy harbour of the Saints,
O sweet and pleasant soil!
In thee no sorrow may be found,
no grief, no care, no toil.

Thy Saints are crowned with glory great;
they see God face to face;
they triumph still, they still rejoice:
most happy is their case.

Jerusalem, Jerusalem,
God grant that I may see

thine endless joy, and of the same
partaker ever be!

PSALMODY

Psalm 51 (50)

Antiphon: *The bones that were crushed shall leap for
joy before the Lord.*

Have mercy on me, God, in your kindness.
In your compassion blot out my offense.
O wash me more and more from my guilt
and cleanse me from my sin.

My offenses truly I know them;
my sin is always before me.
Against you, you alone, have I sinned;
what is evil in your sight I have done.

That you may be justified when you give sentence
and be without reproach when you judge,
O see, in guilt I was born,
a sinner, was I conceived.

Indeed you love truth in the heart;
then in the secret of my heart teach me wisdom.
O purify me, then I shall be clean;
O wash me, I shall be whiter than snow.

Make me hear rejoicing and gladness;
that the bones you have crushed may revive.

From my sins turn away your face
and blot out all my guilt.

A pure heart create for me, O God,
put a steadfast spirit within me.
Do not cast me away from your presence,
nor deprive me of your holy spirit.

Give me again the joy of your help;
with a spirit of fervour sustain me,
that I may teach transgressors your ways
and sinners may return to you.

O rescue me, God, my helper,
and my tongue shall ring out your goodness.
O Lord, open my lips
and my mouth shall declare your praise.

For in sacrifice you take no delight,
burnt offering from me you would refuse,
my sacrifice, a contrite spirit.
A humbled, contrite heart you will not spurn.

In your goodness, show favour to Zion:
rebuild the walls of Jerusalem.
Then you will be pleased with lawful sacrifice,
holocausts offered on your altar.

Glory be to the Father, and to the Son and to the Holy Spirit:
As it was in the beginning, is now, and ever shall be, world without end. Amen.

Antiphon: *The bones that were crushed shall leap for joy before the Lord.*

CANTICLE   *Isaiah 38:10-14, 17-20*

Antiphon: *At the very threshold of death, rescue me, Lord.*

Once I said, "In the noontime of life I must depart!
To the gates of the nether world
I shall be consigned for the rest of my years."
I said, "I shall see the Lord no more in the land of the living.

No longer shall I behold my fellow men among those who dwell in the world."
My dwelling, like a shepherd's tent, is struck down and borne away from me;

You have folded up my life, like a weaver who severs the last thread.
Day and night you give me over to torment; I cry out until the dawn.

155

Like a lion He breaks all my bones;
day and night you give me over to torment.
Like a swallow I utter shrill cries;
I moan like a dove.

My eyes grow weak, gazing heaven-ward:
O Lord, I am in straits; be my surety!
You have preserved my life from the pit of
destruction,
When you cast behind your back all my sins.

For it is not the nether world that gives you
thanks,
nor death that praises you;
Neither do those who go down into the pit await
your kindness.

The living, the living give you thanks, as I do
today.
Fathers declare to their sons, O God, your
faithfulness.

The Lord is our saviour;
we shall sing to stringed instruments
In the house of the Lord all the days of our life.

Glory be to the Father, and to the Son and to the
Holy Spirit.

As it was in the beginning, is now, and ever shall be, world without end. Amen.

Antiphon: *At the very threshold of death, rescue me, Lord.*

Psalm 146 (145)

Antiphon: *I will praise my God all the days of my life.*

My soul, give praise to the Lord;
I will praise the Lord all my days,
make music to my God while I live.

Put no trust in princes,
in mortal men in whom there is no help.
Take their breath, they return to clay
and their plans that day come to nothing.

He is happy who is helped by Jacob's God,
whose hope is in the Lord his God,
who alone made heaven and earth,
the seas and all they contain.

Is it He who keeps faith for ever,
who is just to those who are oppressed.
It is He who gives bread to the hungry,
the Lord, who sets prisoners free.

The Lord, who gives sight to the blind,

who raises up those who are bowed down,
the Lord, who protects the stranger,
and upholds the widow and the orphan.

It is the Lord who loves the just
but thwarts the path of the wicked.
The Lord will reign for ever,
Zion's God, from age to age.

Glory be to the Father, and to the Son and to the
Holy Spirit.
*As it was in the beginning, is now, and ever shall be,
world without end. Amen.*

Antiphon: *I will praise my God all the days of my life.*

READING   *1 Thessalonians 4:14*

If we believe that Jesus died and rose, God will
bring forth with Him from the dead those also
who have fallen asleep believing in Him.

RESPONSORY

I will praise you, Lord, for you have rescued me.
I will praise you, Lord, for you have rescued me.

You turned my sorrow into joy.
I will praise you, Lord, for you have rescued me.
Glory be to the Father, and to the Son and to the
Holy Spirit.

I will praise you, Lord, for you have rescued me.

CANTICLE OF ZECHARIAH
[BENEDICTUS]　　*Luke 1:68-79*

Antiphon: *I am the Resurrection, I am the Life; to believe in me means life, in spite of death, and all who believe and live in me shall never die.*

Blessed be the Lord, the God of Israel;
He has come to His people and set them free.
He has raised up for us a mighty saviour,
born of the house of His servant David.

Through His holy prophets He promised of old
that He would save us from our enemies,
from the hands of all who hate us.
He promised to show mercy to our fathers
and to remember His holy covenant.

This was the oath He swore to our father Abraham:
to set us free from the hands of our enemies,
free to worship Him without fear,
holy and righteous in His sight all the days of our life.
You, my child, shall be called the prophet of the Most High;

159

for you will go before the Lord to prepare His way,
to give His people knowledge of salvation by the forgiveness of their sins.

In the tender compassion of our God
the dawn from on high shall break upon us,
to shine on those who dwell in darkness and the shadow of death,
and to guide our feet into the way of peace.

Glory be to the Father, and to the Son and to the Holy Spirit.
As it was in the beginning, is now, and ever shall be, world without end. Amen.

Antiphon: *I am the Resurrection, I am the Life; to believe in me means life, in spite of death, and all who believe and live in me shall never die.*

INTERCESSIONS

Let us pray to the all-powerful Father who raised Jesus from the dead and gives new life to our mortal bodies, and say to Him:
Lord, give us new life in Christ.
Father, through baptism we have been buried with your Son and have risen with Him in His

resurrection. Grant that we may walk in newness of life so that when we die, we may live with Christ for ever.
Lord, give us new life in Christ.

Provident Father, you have given us the living bread that has come down from heaven and which should always be eaten worthily. Grant that we may eat this bread worthily and be raised up to eternal life on the last day.
Lord, give us new life in Christ.

Lord, you sent an angel to comfort your Son in His agony, give us the hope of your consolation when death draws near.
Lord, give us new life in Christ.

You delivered the three youths from the fiery furnace, free your faithful ones from the punishment they suffer for their sins.
Lord, give us new life in Christ.

God of the living and the dead, you raised Jesus from the dead, raise up those who have died and grant that we may share eternal glory with them.
Lord, give us new life in Christ.

THE LORD'S PRAYER

Our Father, who art in heaven,
hallowed be thy name;
thy kingdom come;
thy will be done on earth as it is in heaven.
Give us this day our daily bread;
and forgive us our trespasses
as we forgive those who trespass against us;
and lead us not into temptation
but deliver us from evil. Amen.

PRAYER

Lord of mercy, hear our prayer.
May our brother/sister.......... whom you called
your son/daughter on earth, enter the kingdom of
peace and light, where your Saints live in glory.
We ask this through our Lord Jesus Christ, your
Son, who lives and reigns with you and the Holy
Spirit, one God for ever and ever.
Amen.

★★★★★

EVENING PRAYER (VESPERS)
INTRODUCTION

O God, come to my aid.
O Lord, make haste to help me.

Glory be to the Father, and to the Son, and to the Holy Spirit.
As it was in the beginning, is now, and ever shall be, world without end. Amen. (Alleluia.)

HYMN

Abide with me, fast falls the eventide
The darkness deepens Lord, with me abide
When other helpers fail and comforts flee
Help of the helpless, oh, abide with me.

Swift to its close ebbs out life's little day
Earth's joys grow dim, its glories pass away
Change and decay in all around I see
O Thou who changest not, abide with me.

I fear no foe, with Thee at hand to bless
Ills have no weight and tears no bitterness
Where is death's sting?
Where, grave, thy victory?
I triumph still, if Thou abide with me.

Hold Thou Thy cross before my closing eyes
Shine through the gloom and point me to the skies

Heaven's morning breaks, and earth's vain shadows flee
In life, in death, o Lord, abide with me.

PSALMODY   *Psalm 121 (120)*

Antiphon: *The Lord will keep you from all evil. He will guard your soul.*

I lift up my eyes toward the mountains:
from where shall come my help?
My help shall come from the Lord,
who made heaven and earth.

May He never allow you to stumble!
Let Him sleep not, your guard.
No, He sleeps not nor slumbers,
Israel's guard.

The Lord is your guard and your shade;
at your right side He stands.
By day the sun shall not smite you,
nor the moon in the night.

The Lord will guard you from evil,
He will guard your soul.
The Lord will guard your going and coming
both now and for ever.

Glory be to the Father, and to the Son and to the Holy Spirit.
As it was in the beginning, is now, and ever shall be, world without end. Amen.

Antiphon: *The Lord will keep you from all evil. He will guard your soul.*

Psalm 130 (129)

Antiphon: *If you kept a record of our sins, Lord, who could escape condemnation?*

Out of the depths I cry to you, O Lord,
Lord, hear my voice!
O let your ears be attentive
to the voice of my pleading.

If you, O Lord, should mark our guilt,
Lord, who would survive?
But with you is found forgiveness:
for this we revere you.

My soul is waiting for the Lord,
I count on His Word.
My soul is longing for the Lord
more than watchman for daybreak.

165

Because with the Lord there is mercy
and fullness of redemption,
Israel indeed He will redeem
from all its iniquity.

Glory be to the Father, and to the Son and to the
Holy Spirit.
As it was in the beginning, is now, and ever shall be,
world without end. Amen.

Antiphon: *If you kept a record of our sins, Lord, who*
could escape condemnation?

CANTICLE   *Philippians 2:6-11*

Antiphon: *As the Father raises the dead and gives*
them life, so the Son gives life to whom He wills.

Though He was in the form of God,
Jesus did not regard equality with God
something to be grasped at.
Rather, He emptied Himself, and took the form
of a slave,
being born in the likeness of men.

He was known to be of human estate,
and it was thus that He humbled Himself,
obediently accepting even death,
death on a cross!

Because of this, God highly exalted Him
and bestowed on Him the name above every
other name.
So that at Jesus' name every knee must bend
in the heavens, on the earth and under the
earth,
and every tongue proclaim to the glory of God
the Father: JESUS CHRIST IS LORD!

Glory be to the Father, and to the Son and to the
Holy Spirit.
*As it was in the beginning, is now, and ever shall be,
world without end. Amen.*

Antiphon: *As the Father raises the dead and gives
them life, so the Son gives life to whom He wills.*

READING   *1 Corinthians 15:55-57*

O death, where is your victory? O death, where
is your sting? The sting of death is sin, and sin
gets its sting from the law. But thanks be to God
who has given us the victory through our Lord
Jesus Christ.

RESPONSORY

Lord, in your steadfast love, give them eternal
rest.
Lord, in your steadfast love, give them eternal rest.

167

You will come to judge the living and the dead.
Give them eternal rest.
Lord, in your steadfast love, give them eternal rest.

Glory be to the Father, and to the Son and to the
Holy Spirit.
Lord, in your steadfast love, give them eternal rest.

CANTICLE OF MARY [MAGNIFICAT]
Luke 1:46-55

Antiphon: *All that the Father gives me will come to
me, and whoever comes to me I shall not turn away.*

My soul proclaims the greatness of the Lord,
my spirit rejoices in God my Saviour
for He has looked with favour on His lowly
servant.

From this day all generations will call me
blessed:
The Almighty has done great things for me, and
holy is His Name.

He has mercy on those who fear Him
in every generation.

He has shown the strength of His arm,
he has scattered the proud in their conceit.
He has cast down the mighty from their thrones
and has lifted up the lowly.

He has filled the hungry with good things,
and the rich He has sent away empty.

He has come to the help of His servant Israel
for He has remembered His promise of mercy,
the promise He made to our fathers,
to Abraham and his children for ever.

Glory be to the Father, and to the Son and to the
Holy Spirit.
As it was in the beginning, is now, and ever shall be,
world without end. Amen.

Antiphon: *All that the Father gives me will come to*
me, and whoever comes to me I shall not turn away.

INTERCESSIONS

We acknowledge Christ the Lord through whom
we hope that our lowly bodies will be made like
His in glory, and we say:
Lord, you are our life and resurrection.

Christ, Son of the living God, who raised up
Lazarus, your friend, from the dead, raise up to
life and glory the dead whom you have
redeemed by your precious blood.
Lord, you are our life and resurrection.

Christ, consoler of those who mourn, you dried
the tears of the family of Lazarus, of the widow's
son, and the daughter of Jairus, comfort those
who mourn for the dead.
Lord, you are our life and resurrection.

Christ, Saviour, destroy the reign of sin in our
earthly bodies, so that just as through sin we
deserved punishment, so through you we may
gain eternal life.
Lord, you are our life and resurrection.

Christ, Redeemer, look on those who have no
hope because they do not know you. May they
receive faith in the resurrection and in the life of
the world to come.
Lord, you are our life and resurrection.

You revealed yourself to the blind man who
begged for the light of his eyes, show your face
to the dead who are still deprived of your light.
Lord, you are our life and resurrection.

When at last our earthly home is dissolved, give us a home, not of earthly making, but built of eternity in heaven.
Lord, you are our life and resurrection.

THE LORD'S PRAYER

Our Father, who art in heaven,
hallowed be thy name;
thy kingdom come;
thy will be done on earth as it is in heaven.
Give us this day our daily bread;
and forgive us our trespasses
as we forgive those who trespass against us;
and lead us not into temptation
but deliver us from evil. Amen.

PRAYER

Lord God, you are the glory of believers and the life of the just. Your Son redeemed us by dying and rising to life again. Your servant .... believed in our own resurrection. Give to him/her the joys and blessings of the life to come. We ask this through our Lord Jesus Christ, your Son, who lives and reigns with you and the Holy Spirit, God for ever and ever.
Amen.

RICHARD III'S REQUESTED COLLECT

O God, whose nature and property is ever to have mercy and to forgive, receive our humble petitions; Be merciful to soul of your servant........ and though we be tied and bound by the chain of our sins yet let the pity of your great mercy loose us.

We ask this through our Lord Jesus Christ, your Son, who lives and reigns with you and the Holy Spirit, God for ever and ever.
Amen.

DISMISSAL
May the Lord bless us and keep us from all evil and bring us to everlasting life.
Amen.

★★★★★

LORD, I WANT ETERNAL LIFE

Thank you Lord
for the gift of my life.
You stood by me
even when I lost my way.
I look all around me
and Your grace is all I see,
I love the life I have,
As I hope for eternal life.

Chorus:
Eternal life, Lord, I want eternal life,
To live with you where the saints behold your face.

Life may have its joy
With some pleasures in this world,
But my hope lies beyond
And my home is far from here.
Teach me my Lord,
To number my length of days,
To keep heaven in mind,
Where my joy will be complete.

I ask you Lord
for the grace to live for you,
Spreading your love
Wherever I find myself.

Loving and caring,
giving and forgiving,
May my life be for your praise
And my death be a great gain.

From dust we came
and to dust shall we return.
Our souls came from you,
For your presence they are made.
Lord, keep my soul from sin,
Let your mercy speak for me.
In the hour of death, help me
May I rest in your kingdom.

Written by
Fr. Emmanuel Gukena Okami

★★★★★

BOOKS BY THE SAME AUTHOR

He Sent Forth His Word, Series 1: Homilies for Sundays, Year A.

He Sent Forth His Word, Series 2: Homilies for Sundays, Year B.

He Sent Forth His Word, Series 3: Homilies for Sundays, Year C.

He Sent Forth His Word, Series 4: Homilies for the Liturgical Seasons of Advent, Christmas, Lent and Easter.

He Sent Forth His Word, Series 5: Homilies for Feasts and Solemnities.

He Sent Forth His Word, Series 6: Homilies for Weekdays, Cycle I.

He Sent Forth His Word, Series 7: Homilies for Weekdays, Cycle II.

A Light to My Path: A Collection of Retreat Talks and Reflections.

His Voice Goes Forth: A Collection of Vocal Meditations and Nuggets.

Lord, Teach Us to Pray: Prayers for Various Occasions.

Pray Without Ceasing: Prayers for Various Occasions.

Seven Days Journey with the Lord: A Handbook for a Self-facilitated Retreat.

Praying with the Psalms.

What God has Joined Together: A Handbook for Marriage Preparation Course.

Whom Shall I Send: A Seven-day Journey with the Lord through His Word.

They Shall be Called My Children: Reflections and Prayers for Children.

When the Spirit Comes Upon You, Series 1: A Nine-day Reflection and Prayers for the Gifts of the Holy Spirit.

When the Spirit Comes Upon You, Series 2:
A Twelve-day Reflection and Prayers for the Fruits
of the Holy Spirit.

When the Spirit Comes Upon You, Series 3:
A Twelve-day Reflection and Prayers for the
Manifestation of the Holy Spirit.

Become a Better Person:
A Thirty-day Journey Towards Self-improvement
and Character Transformation

Vessels for Special Use:
Practical Counsels for Seminarians in Formation

In the Arms of Mary:
Thirty-One Days with Our Blessed Mother
(Fr. Emmanuel Okami and Lisa Timms)

Only Say the Word
365 days of reflection on the Word of God

A Lamp to My Feet
A Collection of Sacred Teachings

He has Done It Before
A Collection of Testimonies of the Power of the
Lord